GAME WARDENS
vs
POACHERS

ADMIT ONE

ADMIT ONE

Tickets Still Available

by
James L. Palmer

Cover Illustration: Phil LaFranka

© 1993 by James Palmer

ISBN: 0-87341-218-4
Library of Congress: 92-74795
Printed in the United States of America

Published by
Krause Publications Inc.
700 E. State St.
Iola, WI 54990
715-445-2214

CONTENTS

PREFACE

In 1957 I was just out of the Air Force and out of work. At the time, $387 a month sounded like a fortune to me, so when I heard the Wisconsin Conservation Department was hiring special conservation wardens and paying them that kind of money, I ran right down and applied. Oh, I liked the idea of working outdoors all right, and it sounded like it might be interesting. But, with apologies to Izaak Walton and Mr. Audubon, it was the money that first attracted me.

I stayed long after I discovered that the wages weren't really so hot after all because I found out it was a lot of fun. I must admit now I harbored no burning desire at the time to protect the state's wildlife from the bad guys. I was just enjoying myself and getting paid for it, too.

Looking back after nearly 30 years, I can't say I've ever seriously regretted doing this for a living. I spent the first 10 years chasing violators around the northwoods and then took a job flying the department's airplanes. I was an undercover warden for a while and eventually wound up as the chief of the special investigations section.

There were days when I felt like a smashing success and was proud of myself. There were other times when I was sure I had been whipped. It was a very exciting job much of the time, and I met some interesting people along the way. Some of them were really nice folks and some of them were knuckleheads.

This book isn't about me. It's about those people I've met and heard about and the events that occurred within eyesight or earshot of me. Some of it I only heard about but have every reason to believe as true. And I just have to tell someone.

Chapter 1

IN SPITE OF
WHAT YOU THOUGHT

First of all, it's important to understand what it's like to be a game warden. In Wisconsin, these people are officially known as conservation wardens. In other states they're called conservation officers, game protectors or conservation police. They prefer to be called game wardens, however.

The game warden is about ten percent conservationist and ninety percent law officer. Most of them, if they weren't good enough to be wardens, would be cops. The big difference between wardens and cops is that the laws wardens enforce deal with wild critters, forests, lakes and fresh air instead of parking meters, pot smokers and purse snatchers. However, the popular characterization of the warden as a gentle naturalist bandaging the leg of an injured baby deer hardly describes most wardens that I knew.

Wardens are spread a lot thinner across the countryside than policemen, so if they are going to be any good at it they must be resourceful and independent. If they are good at it, they make a lot of arrests and a lot of enemies. Those who are timid or lazy don't make many of either. (Yup, folks, like it or not, we keep score on arrests.)

"Arrests," "cases," "tickets" or "pinches" are words commonly used to describe the wardens' product. Their primary job is to catch people who break the game and fish laws. Wardens do, at

5

times, dabble around with hunter education programs, boat safety training and other similar duties, but these are secondary assignments. If a warden is really doing his job, he's writing tickets or making arrests.

In fact, wardens are usually judged by their peers and by their supervisors according to how many and what kind of cases they make. Generally, the more good cases they make, the better wardens they are considered to be.

There are some who take only the easy ones. It is a lot easier and more productive to motor around a lake writing several tickets for improper boat registration than it is to lie out in the woods all night trying to catch an illegal deer hunter. Those who run up a big score by taking only minor violations have learned how to survive in this way of life, but they are little respected. They like to say "a card's a card" or "they're all home runs when they get to Madison." (An arrest card is made out and mailed to the headquarters in Madison for each pinch.)

A genuine, hairy-chested game warden makes several good cases a year. A good case is an illegal fish spearer caught in the middle of the night with a sackful of walleyed pike or a well-known deer poacher captured red-handed. In recent years, a large industrial pollution case can qualify. Such arrests take patience, know-how and courage. The highest compliment one can be paid is to be called a "good warden" by another "good warden."

Because there is only one warden, or maybe two, in a county, they become well known. For this reason the work becomes very personal. The warden is personally offended if a "bandit" (we rarely call them poachers) kills a deer illegally in the warden's area. The bandit probably refers to the warden by his last name rather than by his title as in "there goes that damned Palmer," not "there goes that damned warden."

The result of all of this personalized law enforcement is that many wardens develop very large egos and often work about twice as many hours as the department expects them to work. The public thinks wardens work so many hours because they are dedicated protectors of the wild. In all fairness, some of them are, but more do it out of personal pride. But whatever the reason, the result is a real bargain for the taxpayers who want strict enforcement of the game laws, and a headache for those who choose to violate those laws.

There are about 150 wardens scattered around the state of Wisconsin. Minnesota has about the same — Michigan a few more. There really are not enough in any state. Wardens come in all sizes, styles and shapes. These days they come in both sexes, too.

The selection process is intended to produce only top-quality candidates, and it's working well in modern times. Oh, yes, we do have a few misfits, but what the heck, they're interesting, too.

In the old days, most of us started as assistants or part-time helpers for a real game warden. We were called "specials." That's short for the official designation of Special Conservation Warden. There was, however, little that was special about the job. Specials spent a lot of time alone on "lay jobs" with a walkie-talkie radio. (Lay jobs are what cops call stake-outs.) When an outlaw shot a deer illegally and left it in the woods with plans to return for it later, he usually found a special lying in a clump of brush nearby when he came back. If the special was lucky, he had only been there a short while. Sometimes he had been there for most of a day and a night.

It was also the special's job to change flat tires, gut out the dead deer that were picked up, and keep the real warden's car nice and clean.

If one survived the indignity of being a special, passed the civil service exam and then got lucky, he might become a regular game warden. As a new guy he was still pretty low on the totem pole, but he no longer had to wash dishes or mow the lawn for a real warden.

Today, wardens are well trained. Most of them have a college degree in some natural resources field. And the formal training they receive during their probationary employment period is structured and thorough.

When I started, very few of us were college educated, and the training we received from the department was very spotty. There was little uniformity. We were assigned to work for an experienced warden for training and supervision. One learned whatever the warden decided to teach you. Sometimes that was something useful and sometimes it was something you'd have been better off not knowing. Even under the best wardens, the system was still woefully lacking.

There are some very important academic facts that can elude you under this type of training. When you needed a search warrant before kicking in a door or when you had to read a suspect his rights were things that we learned in action, if at all. I guess the only reason we didn't all wind up on the wrong end of more court cases than we did was because folks simply were not suing each other over every little thing back then.

However, as civil rights activists reared their ugly heads and society became more litigious, we were forced to become better trained and to adopt more professional standards. In just a few years, the social changes which brought on the Miranda warning caused a sharp increase in civil actions against officers. As a result, mandatory training of all law officers became the rule.

During this same period, the Wisconsin Conservation Department was reorganized. Our responsibilities and our authority were more than doubled as all of the environmental issues were added to our bag of tricks. Now, instead of being just a fish and game outfit, we were also citing large corporations for dumping their polluting by-products into the creek. We were now called the Wisconsin Department of Natural Resources. Most states have experienced identical adjustments.

All of this was a dramatic improvement for the citizens, the environment and wildlife. As far as the wardens were concerned, however, things just weren't quite as much fun anymore. Although all of this happened way back in the sixties, whenever I think of "the good old days" as opposed to "modern times," the two eras are delineated by the occasion of these changes.

Still, if you want to be a game warden, Wisconsin is as good a place to be as any. Simply put, there are a lot of resources out there to protect and a bunch of people who tend to abuse these gifts.

A good deal of Wisconsin is heavily wooded and dotted with lakes and marshes. Mink, otter and other fur bearing critters roam the stream banks, and there is a very large deer population spread over the entire state. Wisconsin is centered on a major waterfowl migration route, and the state is bordered north and east by two of the Great Lakes. On the opening day of deer season there may be as many as 500,000 hunters in the woods. A million fishermen could be on the water on a given day. The state's human population of nearly five million includes several thousand trappers, as many bear hunters and several hundred thousand recreational boaters.

A considerable portion of the residents are from rural backgrounds, and there is sort of a pioneer ethic among even the modern-day citizens. Lots of them seem to think that the wildlife was put here for their personal, unregulated use. They have little time for the laws the state legislature has enacted to control the taking of these critters, and none whatsoever for the officers the state has hired to enforce those laws.

How do law violators get that way? Some of them come by it naturally — that is, they are crooks by nature. They may also steal or sell drugs. Many have long criminal records. It's also true that many of them are nice people otherwise. I wound up being downright friendly with some people I'd busted for fairly serious stuff.

My theory is that impatience and peer pressure create many violators. It is said that patience is a virtue. This is especially true for hunters and fishermen. If you're a patient soul who can sit and stare at a red and white bobber floating in the lake for three or four hours, you have the potential to be a good fisherman. There are some skills that you must acquire, and you'll get better after you learn something about fish feeding habits, but you must have the basic ingredient without which no fisherman can excel — patience.

If it means a lot to you to show off some big fish to your buddies and you are impatient by nature, you will likely cheat on the law to do it. I think this is what makes fish and game violators out of otherwise nice folks.

Nearly all of the people we catch are participating in some scheme that takes the waiting, watching or walking out of hunting and fishing. Genuine dyed-in-the-wool bandits come up with some truly ingenious techniques when they are challenged with difficult habitat or wildlife. These guys make a science, maybe even a religion, out of getting more, easier and faster.

Chapter 2

THE DEER SHINERS

"Deer shiners" were Public Enemy No. 1. We considered them the most disgusting of all humans, and catching one was the ultimate deed any warden could do.

If you're not familiar with deer shining, it works like this: Deer are flighty animals and they don't stand around waiting to be pestered. This makes them very difficult to kill, both in season and out. At night, however, a deer will stand still and stare into a bright light shining in its face. The deer is blinded by it and also appears to be fascinated by it. Then, of course, it becomes an easy target. Serious game violators take advantage of the phenomenon. They are called deer shiners. In some parts of the country the terms "jack lighter" or "spotlighter" are used.

Several techniques are commonly used. Traditionally, most shiners work from an automobile. They often drive into small clover or alfalfa fields and sweep the area with either their headlights or a hand-held flashlight. The deer like to feed in these fields at night, and when the beam of light hits them, their eyes glow brightly. When the outlaws kill a deer, they will either throw it in the trunk quickly or they may drop off a cohort to field dress the deer and then return for it later.

Some deer shiners prefer to drive the roads in a very normal manner and at normal speed, watching for deer on the shoulders or in the ditches. They use only the car headlights. When they see a deer they stop, shoot, load the deer in the trunk and drive off, again at a normal rate of speed. The kill takes only seconds and attracts very little attention.

The most difficult shiner to catch is the foot hunter who doesn't use an automobile. He slips quietly into a familiar wooded area. He knows the trails and the feeding areas the deer are most likely to use and can walk to them in total darkness. This is usually a wooded area behind his house.

Foot hunters hunt very late at night and use a small, dim flashlight. They use the light briefly and shoot quickly with a small caliber rifle to keep the noise to a minimum. If they also keep their mouth shut about their violation, they may hunt an entire career and not get caught . . . maybe.

All of these people are hard to catch, and wardens use several methods to nail them. Each method involves hours of waiting to see a light or hear a shot. The waiting is a crashing bore. Everything that happens after seeing the light or hearing the shot is usually exciting as hell.

Nothing makes one feel more like a genuine game warden than catching a good shining "outfit." (Any group of two or more suspects is usually called an "outfit" in warden's parlance.) A "good outfit" means you watched them shoot a deer, load it in the trunk, and when you turned on the red light and siren for the stop, an automobile chase occurred. If they threw the gun out the window at 90 mph (an attempt to get rid of some of the evidence) before you stopped them, or if they tried to run off on foot or wanted to fight, then they were an even better "good outfit." Successfully handling a case such as this was the ultimate trip. It assured you of top status among your peers.

Occasionally you lost the race or the fight and the bad guys got away, in which case you kept it as quiet as possible because . . . oh, well, you have the idea by now, right?

Most of what I knew about catching deer shiners I learned from a warden named Howard DeBriyn, but I never got as good at it as he was. His nickname was "de Bruin" because he resembled a bear, both in appearance and in temperament. He was over six feet tall and weighed well over 200 pounds, most of which was ornery muscle. He had black hair, lots of it. It stuck out of his shirt all the way around his neck, and his arms were long and covered with the growth.

Warden DeBriyn drove a big Oldsmobile and had the uncanny ability to drive the thing without the headlights on, even on the very darkest of nights. Oh, we all drove without lights when it was necessary to catch an outfit, but Howard did it faster, better and more often than anyone else I've ever run into.

He also had a short temper. When an outfit tried to run away from him he would floorboard the big Olds, and when he caught them he didn't bother to let up on the gas pedal. He referred to this as "giving them a little nudge." It usually meant new grille parts and headlights for the Olds and considerable body work to the rear half of the fleeing car.

Howie was the first warden I was assigned to work for, and one of the first things that happened was we caught a really "good outfit."

It was a cold October night, and the rain had been coming down for two or three days. My boss dropped me off on the edge of a little ten-acre clover field that the shiners had been periodically working over. We had worked this case for several nights, and I knew I was in for a long, lonely wait. Rarely did a car even drive past the little field, and three deer grazed peacefully back near the woods line each evening.

I wore rubber boots and a good rain parka. Warden DeBriyn had given me his best binoculars and a portable two-way radio. There was no place near the field to get the Oldsmobile out of sight, so Howie drove north a mile and a half and backed the car onto a little logging road. There he threw some branches over the front of his car. My orders were that I should hunker down in the brush on the edge of the field and wait to see who might show up. If an outfit worked the field, I was to call him on the radio with the details and he would come roaring out of his den and handle the apprehension.

I hunkered long into the miserable night, shivering in the cold rain. I played games to keep my mind off my misery. I devised a guessing game where I'd try to check my watch only once an hour, on the hour. I was pretty close the first couple hours. Eventually I had to abandon the game, a loser. I was so cold I lost all sense of time and swore that my watch was running about ten minutes to the hour. My shoulders ached from hunching them up to keep the rain from running down my neck. I wondered if Howie was standing outside his car, just as cold and wet as I was. I wondered why I hadn't gone back to college that fall instead of becoming a special.

At last a rattly old DeSoto came up the road and pulled into the field. I could see a single occupant as the old car rolled past me. He drove to the center of the opening and slowly began circling, sweeping the little field with his headlights.

The car jerked to a stop as its lights found the three deer in a corner of the field. Within seconds a rifle barrel poked out the car window. Suddenly the quiet night was shattered by a flash of fire and a great boom. The biggest deer dropped dead. The others high-tailed it for the woods. The man was out of the car and running to his kill before the other deer were out of sight. He returned to the DeSoto and loaded the carcass into the trunk. The whole process took less than two minutes.

I sent an excited message to Howie on the radio and took off on the run for the road. Within five steps I tripped on an old piece of barbed wire fence and fell flat on my face. My armload of equipment was lost in the long grass. I started searching for it, but my flashlight was gone, too, and I wasn't having much luck. I could hear Warden DeBriyn's car tearing down from the north on the gravel road, so I forgot the gear and raced out to the road without it.

The Oldsmobile slid to a stop long enough for me to jump in, and we were off at nearly 90 mph with no headlights. Up ahead about a mile, a pair of dim taillights showed. In a voice that had none of the tremble of mine, my boss asked, "Is that the guy that shot?" I wondered if my voice shivered because I was so cold and wet or if I was that nervous. I looked over at him to see if he was wet, but it was too dark to tell.

I told him that the taillights up ahead probably belonged to our customer. As we careened down the narrow road with gravel drumming up on the inside of the fenders, he calmly listed all the mistakes I had made in the past few minutes. I wished he would forget about me and pay more attention to the road. He said I should have told him on the radio which way the car had gone and described it for him, instead of whatever it was that I had said. That way he wouldn't have had to stop for me and the guy would probably be in handcuffs by now. I couldn't see any point in telling him that his binoculars and radio were lying back there somewhere.

The old gray DeSoto was no match for the big Olds 98. We were behind it in minutes. Howard turned on the headlights and siren when we were about twenty feet behind the old heap. The driver didn't stop. He moved over to the middle of the road and accelerated to about 70 mph, which appeared to be top end for the old clunker.

The rifle flew out the window and crossed the ditch towards the woods. Howie snatched my hat off my head and threw it out the window onto the road. I learned later that he was marking the spot so that we would be able to locate the gun. He never did explain why he used my hat instead of his own. (Are you getting a feel for the role of a special?)

The chase continued south towards the county line. Up ahead the road made a slight bend to the left. Warden DeBriyn announced that the race was over. He tromped on the gas pedal and drove into the rear end of the outlaw's car, pushing it out of the curve and off the road. I watched with fascination as the old sedan burst through the center of a big signboard that read, "Copenhagen, the tasty way to take tobacco."

It took only a few seconds to locate the car in a big patch of hazelnut brush, but we were too late. The driver's door stood open and there was no one around. Howie recognized the car though, and he knew who our deer shiner was. His name was Ellington and he had several previous game-law convictions. He was a tough hombre who always ran and always fought.

DeBriyn said the guy would probably head straight for home. He lived about three miles away, and a lot of swampy river bottom had to be crossed to get there.

Slowly, quietly and without lights we drove east and hid Howard's car in the woods about half a mile from Ellington's mailbox. Then we hid in the road ditch that ran past the house. Howie was about a hundred yards east of the mailbox and I was as far to the west.

Here I was, hunkering again. We hunkered for nearly two hours as the temperature dropped a few degrees and the rain turned into snow. By this time I was colder than I had ever been in my life and shivering uncontrollably. I wished I had my cap. I supposed that resignation was out of the question at the moment. I was beginning to wonder how a person ended one of these deals.

Then I heard a sound in the woods close to me. My heart was hammering so loud I was sure Ellington would hear it as he walked towards me. Damn it, I wished he had come out near Howard instead. I could see Ellington now. He was limping slightly and steam spurted from his nose and mouth when he panted for breath. He looked like a swamp monster from a horror movie. He looked mighty big, too. He rounded the last clump of brush that separated us. Apprehensively, I stood up in front of him and announced that I was a game warden and that he was under arrest.

He took off running just as Howie had said he would. He sped down through the ditch and out onto the road and turned towards his house. I caught him near the mailbox, and when I tackled him we slid down the wet gravel road for ten feet. We got to our feet and he struggled to get loose. We sort of wrestled our way down the road. He was so exhausted from his travels that he couldn't make much trouble. I was so weak from shivering and hunkering that I wouldn't have been able to do much about it if he had. Once in a while one of us would let go with one hand and take a swing at the other. We mostly shoved, fell, got up, hung on, and pushed on one another. I was trying to transfer the struggle down the road towards Warden DeBriyn.

It was a tremendous relief when my boss stepped out of the ditch, dumped Ellington on his face and handcuffed him. I was sort of proud of myself until Howie, without stifling the laugh, asked us where in hell we took our dancing lessons.

We loaded our cold, wet deer shiner in the car and drove back to his abandoned heap. The keys were in his pocket, and when we unlocked the trunk we found that I had watched this outlaw kill his third deer of the evening. Several miles away we found my cap in the road and a .300 Savage rifle in the woods nearby.

Ellington plead guilty in Price County Court the next morning and sat in jail most of the winter because he couldn't raise enough money to pay his fine. Howie probably will never know, unless he reads this, that I sneaked back out to the little clover field that morning and recovered his radio, binoculars, and what was left of my reputation.

I only worked for Howie for two months but I developed a lot of respect for him. I'm sure that I decided to try to become a full-time warden as a result of our association. He struggled with a pencil and paper and hated to do his reports. They were never very neat and several words might be spelled incorrectly, but he had all of the common sense in the world and a great knowledge of human nature. He also knew how to catch violators. As the saying goes, "He had a nose for business."

One day Howie asked me if I could type. I said, "No." He said, "Well, you'd better learn fast because I want you to do these arrest cards." Arrest cards are really simple. All you had to put on them was the defendant's name and address, the date of the arrest, what the charge was, how much the guy was fined and a couple of other details. It was strictly a fill-in-the-blanks deal. He gave me half a dozen to do, in triplicate.

I started hunting and pecking my way through them. I made several mistakes and had to start over. I wanted these to be letter perfect. I'd heard enough criticism from this guy and he wasn't going to find anything wrong here if I could help it. Finally, I had the first one completed and noticed that I'd spent over half an hour on it. I felt that I had to speed the job up or I was going to catch hell for being slow. I tried to work faster but that just generated more mistakes. The morning flew by as I toiled over the ancient old Underwood. In spite of my determination, there were several carbon smudges and eraser scrapes on them. Finally, just before noon, I took the cards to him. Any first-year typing student would have had it done in twenty minutes. He accepted them with a grunt.

I tried hard to please Howard. He wasn't one to pass out compliments, and I never knew where I stood with him. Never knew, that is, until one day late in November. There were five or six wardens, including Howie and me, staying in a shack down on the county line. We were working deer shiners every night and grouse hunters in the daytime.

One evening, just before supper, they started a card game. I didn't have any money to lose so I seized the opportunity to catch a few winks of shut-eye before the night shift on shiners went out. I flopped out across a bunk and was sleeping in a few seconds.

After an hour or so I woke and was just lying there, half listening to the conversation at the card table. One of the other wardens asked Howie, "Is that new special of yours any good?" Howie said, "You're damned right he is, and, boy, is he a whiz on a typewriter."

Everyone who worked for DeBriyn has a story to tell. One of the more popular is told about a guy named Elmer Lewan. Elmer "specialed" for Howie one fall, and the next year he was working for Warden Ed Hill in Sawyer County. One day Ed got a call about a dead bear lying in a field outside town. He and Elmer drove out to investigate.

They decided that some shiner had mistaken the bear's glowing eyes for a deer the previous night. After they shot it and discovered it was a bear, they didn't know what to do with it, so they just let it lie. As was the custom, Ed handed a knife to Elmer and said, "Gut it out." Elmer rolled the bear over on its back and bent to the task. Suddenly he straightened up and said, "I just can't do it, Ed."

"What do you mean, you can't do it?" Hill asked.

Elmer said, "It looks too much like Howie, and Howie is my hero. I just can't do it."

Warden John McGaver tells about the time he and Howard had been to a meeting together. On the way home they stopped in a tavern for a beer. Howie had been bragging to John all fall about how he could gut out a deer in 40 seconds. He repeated the boast again in the bar. After about four beers they got in the car and started down the road towards home.

A few miles out of town a deer darted out of the ditch right in front of the car ahead of them. The driver jammed on the brakes and swerved but was unable to avoid the animal. The big doe was dead but appeared to be salvageable, as there were no visible injuries except for a broken neck. The wardens identified themselves, took the driver's name and sent him on. Then Howie suggested that John gut it out and haul it into town. John said, "Oh, no, Howie, you gut it out. And do it in 40 seconds."

Howie agreed that this was as good a time as any to show the upstart what an old-time warden could do. He took off his new Harris tweed sport coat and laid it gently in the clean snow on the shoulder of the road, rolled up his sleeves and told John to get out his watch and time him.

When the second hand was straight up, McGaver hollered, "Go!" and DeBriyn went to work. The knife blade flashed in the moonlight as a few deft cuts reamed the rear end of the dead deer and then laid its body cavity open. With no lost motion he reached up in the front of the rib cage and loosened the lungs and heart.

Two more slashes and Howie tossed the knife on the ground and reached in with both hands to remove the entire innards of the deer in one pull.

John glanced at his watch and saw that barely 30 seconds had passed as Howard straightened up with both hands full of 40 pounds of steaming, bloody wet guts. Warden DeBriyn triumphantly hollered, "Time!" and tossed the guts . . . right on top of his new sport coat.

Back in those times, before the department expanded to handle environmental matters, wardens in the northern third of the state seemed to spend about half their time on deer shiners. During the busiest season, which usually started about the Fourth of July, we rarely knocked off before 3 o'clock in the morning. We worked, talked, ate and dreamed deer shiners. This meant that about eight hours, out of however many you decided to work that day, were worked in darkness.

In the early 1960s, a high percentage of our shiners were hunting along major highways. A lot of new highways had been built up north, and part of that process included seeding the shoulders with a seed that produced a good cover crop of grass to prevent erosion of the recent grading. Whatever that stuff was, the deer were wild about it. It was common to see literally hundreds of deer in a 20-mile stretch of highway. The outlaws would wait until the traffic had cleared (usually half an hour after the bars closed), and then they would drive along waiting for the right deer in the right place. When they spotted one that wasn't near any homes and there were no other cars in sight, they would stop and blast it. They would load the deer and be off again in a matter of seconds.

We caught very few of those guys by sitting in one spot and waiting for them to shoot a deer in front of us. The best method was to pick out a car that looked suspicious and slip in close behind it with our lights off. We would tail it several miles until the driver either passed up a few deer in the right locations and convinced us he wasn't hunting, or he shot one.

Often we would drive a couple hundred miles in one night on a stretch of road twenty miles long, never turning the headlights on. We caught a lot of outfits this way. We also banged up a lot of cars. Several wardens told me how they had followed 20 yards behind suspects' autos at 50 mph and had seen deer run across the road between the two vehicles. Nearly all of us wound up, at least once, going into the ditch at high speed.

Although we've had a few wardens killed and others badly hurt in vehicle accidents, I don't recall ever hearing that we lost one while tailing a shiner up close. I'll give Lady Luck the credit on that one. I never would have admitted it at the time, but towards the end of the fall, after five months of this, night after night, I used to get a little punchy.

Sometimes the arrest itself got pretty hairy. All of those deer shiners had guns with them, and none of them were ever very happy to see us. Most of the time they were reasonable, but occasionally a surly one would really test you. Not surprisingly, our arrest plan invariably called for getting the guns out of their hands and into ours just as quickly as possible. More than one warden wound up looking down the barrel of one from the wrong end.

There is an old joke that circulates around the force every few years, and it goes something like this. A new special asks his boss, "What do I do if somebody points his gun at me?" The warden replies, "Don't worry about it, kid, the guy with the gun will tell you exactly what to do."

In fact, what usually happens is that the warden does a lot of fast talking and edges up close enough so that if the guy isn't talked into giving up the gun, the warden can make a fast grab. They will then share joint possession of the gun briefly, until the warden pulls one of several practiced dirty tricks that should result in sole possession forfeited to our side. It usually works, but some wardens have been shot, too.

There are also some very subtle perils included in deer shining operations. One that comes to mind — and that always makes me smile — never makes Henry Kern smile.

Henry was my neighbor warden to the south. We worked together a lot and it was usually fun. He wasn't very big, but he had as much nerve as anybody in the outfit.

Folks who broke the game laws often challenged him because he was of challengeable size and because his attitude might have invited it a little. He had some awful scraps, including one long, dragged-out battle that he thought he wouldn't survive. Hank wound up flat on his back with the bad guy sitting on him. The crook had Kern's binocular strap twisted around Henry's neck and was strangling him. Just before the lights went out, Hank managed to get out his revolver and club the guy on the head and face with it enough times to discourage him. Henry then got the upper hand, and the outlaw lost an eye and spent a year in the state prison.

That isn't the event that makes me smile. I always smile about the evening Hank was working shiners west of the small town where he was stationed. He was parked in the woods, on the edge of a big alfalfa field. Deer had been feeding there regularly, and Warden Kern noticed fresh tire tracks turning into the field. He figured the chances were pretty good that the tracks were being made by a vehicle with a rifle and a flashlight in it. As it turned out, he was right.

He found a handy place to back his car into the woods where it would be out of sight. The only problem with the spot was that it was a little lower than the field and a car driving in the field would occasionally drop out of sight.

After spending a few nights on the case and drinking gallons of coffee, it finally happened. The bad guys arrived in an old Studebaker pickup. They pulled off the road and into the field. The passenger got in the box of the truck and leaned over the top of the cab as the truck started to slowly circle the field. Henry grabbed his binoculars and glassed the outfit just as their lights picked up the reflection from the eyes of a herd of deer. Hank told his special that he could see a rifle in the hands of the guy in the truck box.

The deer were about 200 yards ahead of the truck. The driver slowly eased the Studebaker straight towards them. But just about the time it was approaching shooting range, the truck disappeared into a slight depression.

Hank jumped up on the trunk of his car and, standing on tip toes, could just see the outfit. He was standing right next to the mobile police-band radio antenna. The antenna was a solid piece of spring steel about four feet long that resembled a rapier.

When the guy shot, Warden Kern had a good view of the action. Apparently, the shot missed. All of the deer scattered at top speed and headed for cover. Hank had seen enough. He and his special could both testify that the crew was hunting. They had a case. All they had to do was put the grab on them.

The truck turned and started out of the field. Kern said, "Let's take 'em," and stepped off the trunk to drop to the ground. Just as his feet cleared the vehicle, the tip of the antenna entered his left nostril. Even in the pitch darkness he realized what had happened. It was still three feet to the ground and he was already having visions of the sharp steel tip going up into his brain. As he fell, he heaved himself backwards in an attempt to get free. Gravity was doing its thing, however, and when he hit the ground the aerial was bent in a big half circle which still terminated in his nose.

He jumped and danced up and down trying to get unhooked and relieve the pressure and pain. When he was finally free, he fell to the ground bleeding and in agony. By the time he got the bleeding stopped and figured out that he was going to survive, the outlaws' truck was miles away. Not many deer shiners got a free shot on Hank Kern, but that one did.

When you spend a good share of your nights prowling around the country with your headlights out, you sneak up on some strange things. Over the years, game wardens have found countless runaway kids, stolen cars, stranded motorists and even a few corpses. They have also interrupted a few burglaries and lots of lovemaking.

In 1962, I was transferred to Superior, located in the northwest corner of the state. By northern Wisconsin standards, Superior was a big city. I patrolled about 700 square miles of the surrounding area. There were a lot of deer there, and a lot of outlaws hunting them.

John Chapin was the warden in Hayward, a busy tourist center about 60 miles southeast of Superior. John was a bachelor with few interests outside his work, and he spent nearly every waking hour on the job. Hayward was a good place for a guy like John because there was a lot for a game warden to do there.

The deer shiners were really shooting up his county one fall. He was catching outfits periodically, but there seemed to be little deterrent effect to his successes. He asked me to come down and give him a hand for a few nights.

John planned to work north of Round Lake where a gang was killing a deer a week. He also had a complaint from a farmer that someone else was shining almost every night, about ten miles southwest of the first spot. He wanted me to work the south complaint. We would be in radio contact in case either of us needed help.

On the first night, things were slow on my end of the project. We visited on the radio every hour or so, just to stay awake. About every other time he called, John told me about some action he had just had. He had followed several cars and had stopped one. The occupants turned out to be some "lookers." Lookers were nice folks out driving around looking at the pretty deer. When we stopped them and found no guns in the car, they always smiled and said, "We're just looking." John had also heard two shots north of him, but they were too far away to do anything about. The night wore on slowly, and I heard and saw nothing.

Sometime after midnight, I got a call from Warden Chapin and his voice sounded a little tense. He said he had followed another carload of suspects and they had shot a deer right in front of him. He was now chasing them at over a hundred miles per hour and it didn't appear as though they planned to stop. He figured they were heading for Hayward, and he wanted me to start that way and try to get ahead of the chase to block them.

I did, just as fast as my Ford would go. Before I was halfway there, John called again and said that he had their car stopped and things were going pretty well. He was taking them to the county jail and he wouldn't need my help after all. I cursed my luck for missing out on all of the fun and returned to my parking spot.

Later, after John had locked up his deer shiners and it was almost sunup, he drove down to where I was sitting. We visited for a spell and then called the operation off for the night. I was surprised when Chapin said he had a passenger who needed a ride to Superior. I asked him where he had found the guy, but John just said, "He'll probably tell you about it." I told the stranger to get in and I started for home.

He was just a kid — a skinny, scared-looking kid. I guessed he was about eighteen. Although the temperature was in the 20s, he wore only jeans and a T-shirt. Not only did he have no coat, but he was barefoot as well. He smelled sort of sweet and funny and there was something red all over his face and shirt. It goes without saying that he was nearly frozen. He was pretty quiet at first, but it was 60 miles to Superior and he finally opened up.

He was, it turned out, a freshman at the university in Superior. He was being initiated into a fraternity and that was the source of his problem. He told how his "brothers" had blindfolded him, taken his shoes and most of his clothes, bundled him into a car and had driven for over an hour before dumping him out. Before they left they taped his wrists together behind his back, taped his mouth shut and smeared lipstick all over him. He had no idea where in hell he was, but somehow he was supposed to find his way back to the dormitory before breakfast and report in to them.

He told me that when a car came down the road, he would run out in front of it and turn his back towards it so that the driver could see his hands were bound and he needed help. The first two or three cars drove around him and continued on into the night.

After what he thought was probably about two hours, Chapin stopped his car alongside the kid, peeled off the tape and listened to his tale of woe. The kid was tickled pink to discover that John was a law officer and that he had been rescued. But the poor kid's terrifying evening had just begun.

John wasn't about to call off our project because of some college kid's predicament. He stuck the freshman in the back seat and went back to working deer shiners. For hours they sped up and down the back roads with no lights on. They followed other cars for miles in total darkness. John stopped other cars with the emergency red lights flashing and the siren wailing away. Then the kid watched in horror as a deafening roar and a ball of fire in the night spelled death for Bambi's mom. The 110-mph automobile race which followed was almost more than his nerves could handle. When the warden jammed two handcuffed, half-drunk thugs in the back seat with him and motored off to jail, the boy began to wish that Chapin had driven around him and disappeared into the night, just as the drivers before him had done.

He talked a bit about his college courses, social life on the campus and his future. I asked him what his career plans were. He said, "I can tell you one thing that I sure as hell don't want to be. I ain't going to be a damned game warden!"

It was ten minutes to eight when I dropped him off in front of his dormitory. He forgot to thank me for the ride.

One rainy night we were working three cars on deer shiners in Payson County. Again, I was helping out a neighboring warden stationed several miles east of me. There was a long section of new highway that had just been opened to traffic. The deer had found the new seeding and so had the deer shiners. We were doing our thing, following suspects up and down the road with the lights off. With three warden's cars spaced about fifteen miles apart, we added a variation to the technique.

Warden Kale Brown was parked on the east end of the project, Ken Buckley was in the middle, and I was on the west end. If I tailed a car east, I would drop off just before I came to Buckley's spot and then he would pull in behind the suspect outfit and follow it to where Kale sat. It worked just as well in the opposite direction. If we made a stop, we planned to do it between cars so that if we got a runner there was someone up the road a few miles to do a block. Traffic was extremely light and nearly every motorist got an invisible escort through the deer area.

About two hours before daylight, we had absolutely nothing to show for our efforts. The conversation over the mobile radio became a discussion of the merits of giving up for the night.

Buckley suggested that we get together in one car to drain our thermos bottles and plan the next night's work. We did. Three big wardens, bundled up in thick down-filled jackets, were crammed into the front seat of my Ford when a set of headlights approached from the west. The car was traveling slowly and weaved slightly every half mile or so, causing the headlight beams to shine across the ditches.

This was the best-looking prospect that had been past all night. I fired up and swung in behind it. After a few miles it became apparent that the guy was weaving due to a high blood alcohol level and that he wasn't hunting at all.

We decided to drop him, and Buckley told me that there was a driveway about a half mile ahead where I could back in and we could finish our palaver. As I backed in, I noticed a small house that was served by the driveway. When I came even with the house, there was a loud whang as the steel antenna mounted on my roof hit the power wires leading to the house. It made a hell of a racket and, in the moonlight, I could see the wires swinging violently back and forth. I wondered aloud if I hadn't awakened everybody in the house. Buckley said that he knew the people and had their permission to hide his car in their driveway when he worked the area.

We sat there for only a moment when a light in the house came on. We had stopped right even with, and about five feet from, a window. Within minutes, a woman appeared at the window. She stood sideways to us and seemed to be facing a mirror. She fussed with her curly red hair and then began to pat some powder on her nose and her fat cheeks. We could see only the upper half of her. She was about fifty years old and a bit overweight. She wore only a brassiere.

My first thought was to sneak out of there with the lights off before the poor woman noticed us. I voiced that notion out loud and Kale agreed with me. Buckley said, "Stay right where you are." The car door slammed shut and Buckley was gone. She removed the bra. Kale and I sat fascinated as she began vigorously brushing her teeth. Everything shook. Suddenly, she turned towards the rear of the house as though she had heard something. A big smile creased her fat face as she hurried from our view. Just before the lights went out, we could see the shadow of two people on the wall.

It was nearly an hour later and starting to show a little light in the eastern sky when the lights in the house came on again. A short time later, Ken got back in the car without a word. He had brought with him a big plate heaped with cookies. We drove off in silence. They were oatmeal cookies — my favorite.

Chapter 3

THE FISH PIRATES

The walleyed pike is probably the premier fish in Wisconsin's inland waters. The muskie, the northern pike and the sturgeon all get a lot bigger. They, along with the bass, are also considered better fighters on a rod and reel. Some people will tell you that several different kinds of panfish taste just as good as walleyes. Trout fishermen are apt to tell you anything. Still, the walleye seems to be the most sought after by the most people.

Good fishermen, who otherwise appear to be perfectly normal, will sit for hours in a cold, ugly rain for a bag limit of pike. They will stand out on the frozen surface of one of the state's 10,000 lakes in sub-zero weather and break ice in an eight-inch hole for half the night, just to take four or five home with them.

The "pirates," of course, have a better idea. They have devised several schemes for catching lots of pike with a minimum of effort. The wardens, for their part, have devised several schemes for catching the pirates catching the walleyes. It gets to be almost like a game, but a very serious one.

Spearing the spawning run is a very popular method for getting them the easy way. The walleyes spawn about the same time that the frogs start chirping in the spring. When the leaves on a plum tree are about the size of a squirrel's ear, the water temperature in most nearby lakes and streams will be just about right to arouse the sexual desire in the pike.

They spawn on gravel creek beds or gravel bars in the lakes. Just like most other critters (including people), they like to do it at night and are very determined about it. So determined, in fact, that the otherwise wary buggers do not desist when you walk in among them and start jabbing them with a spear, a pitchfork, or swatting them with the jack handle out of your trunk. They can even be taken by hand in shallow water. It's easy, it's against the law, and it's against the peace and dignity of the state of Wisconsin.

The gill nets used by commercial fishermen are also very effective on these fish. They, too, are illegal. So are the fish traps that are in common use during the spawning run. The trap is usually made of chicken wire. It is simply a large holding cage which is often cylindrical and may be any size, depending on the manufacturer's degree of optimism. The thing all fish traps have in common is a funnel-shaped entrance that is easy for a fish to swim into, but hard to swim out of. They are placed in the stream with the entrance on the downstream end. Fish naturally traveling upstream move freely into them. Really clever bandits will put a ripe female pike in the trap for bait.

I don't mean to imply that the pirates don't cheat on other species of fish besides the walleye, because they do. There are also dozens of other unlawful tricks and paraphernalia used by these guys. The set-liners, the dynamiters and the electric fishermen are just as effective.

I wish that Fred and I had been better friends. It's not that we were unfriendly, because we weren't. We shared similar interests. We were both competitive pistol shooters; he was a little bit better than I was. We were both pilots; I was better than he was. Because we were both too serious about this stuff, we just never got to be real good friends. Game wardens can be sort of childish about things like that.

I had a lot of respect for him, but I was careful not to let it show. And if he had any for me, he was doing the same thing.

After an active tour as a field warden, Fred was promoted to warden supervisor in one of the areas in the northern part of the state. Those guys had a tough job. They had to direct and supervise eight or ten field wardens who were very independent by nature. Most field wardens also resent criticism in any form.

In addition to this monumental task, supervisors were expected to set a good example by having an effective enforcement program (pinch a bunch of people) of their own. I always figured Fred had about the biggest bunch of hardheads to supervise in the outfit. Life must have been hard sometimes.

He was a talented guy who did a lot of things well. However, nobody is perfect, and Fred was impulsive. He didn't always plan ahead as far as he should have, and once in a while he wound up in an uncomfortable situation. That's what happened one spring when he was working on some fish pirates.

The phone rang in the office. A "snitch" was on the line, wanting to talk to the supervisor. The snitch told Fred about a gill net that was stretched across a little creek in a remote corner of Fred's area. Gill netting was bad outlawing, and the warden supervisor was really interested. The guy knew right where it was. He told.

Netters and trappers usually run their gear after dark. I suppose they think there is less chance of being caught then. No warden worth his salt sits around watching TV after supper during the fish run.

Late in the afternoon, Fred drove out and stashed his car out of sight off a logging road and hiked a mile through the brush to the creek where the net was supposed to be. It took a while to locate it. It had been set by someone who knew what he was doing. The net lines were tied to some underwater roots. There were no floats on top of the net to give it away. It was simply pulled tight across the narrow creek. There were already a dozen walleyes hung up in the sheet of net.

31

Being careful not to leave any telltale tracks in the mud, he backed away several feet and stood looking around for a spot where he could hide. He wanted to be certain that he was far enough away so as not to be found, but close enough to see clearly when the net was fished.

The creek wound its way through a little meadow at this point. There was no brush cover for several hundred yards along the creek. There was a clump of spruce trees about 50 yards back from the net. That, he thought, might be a good spot. A closer look revealed a neat little cottage nestled back in the spruce grove. It was painted green and was difficult to spot from the creek.

He circled the building and noted that all of the windows were shuttered. For all appearances the place had not been used in some time. He found one shutter that was not fastened and tried the window. It was unlocked, so he crawled in.

He found that he had an excellent view of the creek from the window and decided that it was probably OK for a warden supervisor to enter a building that had an unlocked window if it was purely in the line of duty. He looked around and saw that the cabin was kept up very well and was neat as a pin. This was, he decided, a good place to hide and wait out his pirates. He pulled a chair over by the window and made himself comfortable.

In an hour or so, something began to stir in Fred. At first it was just an uneasy feeling, but it soon became a heavy sensation in the pit of his stomach. It had nothing to do with the gill net. It had to do with the four tacos he had for lunch. The sense of fullness grew until he suffered cramps and felt as though he would burst. There was no longer any question about it. He was going to have to answer nature's call promptly — in fact, immediately.

He looked through the cottage and found that there was no bathroom, but he hadn't thought there would be. He recalled seeing an old-fashioned outhouse a little farther back in the spruce trees. It was dusk now and his gill netters could arrive any minute. The outhouse was a poor option, as it put him in a spot where he couldn't see the creek. He also didn't want to get spotted outside the building if his suspects arrived at the wrong time. Besides, he didn't believe he would survive the journey anyway. There was now only one option.

He grabbed an old newspaper that was lying on the table and spread it out on the living room floor. He removed his heavy gun belt, laid it on the table and dropped his gray uniform trousers down around his ankles. Squatting over the newspaper, he experienced the wonderful sensation of complete relief. It was then that he heard a car door slam.

He ran to the front door and peered through the curtains. Two men were walking down the path towards the front door. One was fumbling in his pocket for something. He came out with a key. They were acting as if they belonged there, and Fred was beginning to feel as if he didn't. Did they own the place? Were they the gill netters? It really didn't matter now. It was clear that they were coming in.

Fred made a dash for the window, nearly stepping in the steaming remains of the object of his relief. That would have to go with him. As he was rolling up the newspaper, he could hear the key sliding in the lock. Quickly he ducked through the window and eased it shut just as the front door swung open. He darted around behind the wood pile and knelt out of sight. There he was — shooting champion, pilot, one of Wisconsin's finest, dressed in the perfectly tailored gray gabardine uniform of a conservation warden supervisor, hiding behind a wood pile with a wad of dung under his arm.

He felt a little silly at first and then real panic gripped him as remembered that his .357 magnum revolver, fully loaded, of course, was lying on the table in the same room with the two unknown subjects.

His mind was racing. He could hear the men talking in hushed tones, but couldn't make out the words. He imagined that they were trying the heft of his pistol, or examining his handcuffs, or marveling at the ingenious little speed loaders full of more ammunition. Each year, a few law officers are killed with their own sidearms. Fred wondered if it had ever happened just like this before.

He began wondering how the press release would read. How would it explain the damp, warm, weakening bundle under his arm? He set it down and inched a few feet away from it.

He heard the door slam and now the voices were much louder. They were outside. Peering over the woodpile, he found no one in sight. Frantically, he sprinted back to the window and dove in. There, just as he had left it, lay his gun belt. The pistol was still in the holster. The other equipment was undisturbed. How could they have missed it? The aroma was still strong in the room. How in hell did they ever miss that? Incredible as it seemed, the evidence of his intrusion had gone unnoticed.

Now his confidence returned in a rush. He hurried to the window and looked down towards the creek. The two men were dragging the net up onto the stream bank. He could see the sleek, fat walleyes flopping in the grass.

Calmly, he strapped on his gun belt, exited again and crept down towards the creek. In the gathering darkness, he moved to within a few feet of the busy men. With a quiet confidence, honed by years of professional enforcement experience, he confronted the outlaws.

They were, it turned out, hardened violators with lengthy records of fish and game law convictions. For years they had been offending society with selfish violations that anger honest sportsmen everywhere. Now, they would be brought to justice. Once again, the long arm of modern law enforcement triumphed over greed and evil.

At their court appearance, they quietly pleaded guilty and paid the maximum fines. I guess they never will know all of what went on in their cottage that evening.

When I became a regular, full-time warden, my first assignment was in Jefferson County. Jefferson is in the southern part of the state. I'd never been there before. The place was foreign to me. The resources were different and the people were different. There were a lot fewer trees down there and a lot more people, buildings and automobiles. Of course, the violators' techniques were also different.

The warden I was replacing was Bill Laesch. He had been in Jefferson for 20 years. He was a wiry, little guy, barely tall enough to make the five-foot, eight-inch height requirement for wardens. He was also a really nice guy. His health wasn't good and he had no obligation to help me get started. He was retired but he took the time to show me the ropes. He made my transfer to what northern wardens derisively called the "banana belt" a whole lot easier.

The first thing I learned was that Bill had a heck of a good reputation, and the locals doubted that some new kid from up north could fill his shoes. Nearly everyone I met had a story to tell about Bill. He was crafty.

Where I came from, fish pirates almost always speared their fish. A walleyed pike's eyes glow in the dark like a deer's eyes if you shine a light on them. Up north, the water was clear and the fish were an easy target. Down south, there were very few walleyes and the water was too dirty to see them. The pirates used fish traps and they caught more white bass and rough fish than anything else. I had heard a lot about fish traps, but I had never seen one. Bill said he would show me how to locate them and how to catch the operators.

One Saturday morning, we put the boat in the Rock River south of Fort Atkinson. Bill now wore civilian clothes and I put an old hunting coat on over my uniform so that people wouldn't know what we were up to. We started downstream towards Lake Kosh-konong. Wherever a feeder creek dumped into the Rock, Bill would tell me to slow up and idle past the mouth. He had a little drag hook on a light rope that he lowered into the water. We checked several likely spots in this manner. Within ten minutes, he snagged a trap. We pulled it up alongside the boat. The fish in it were dead and it was full of weeds, abandoned. A fellow could waste the rest of his life waiting for someone to fish it.

The last mile or so of the river, before it dumps into the lake, runs along a strip of land called Blackhawk Island. Here, houses and summer cottages line the west shore of the river. Bill explained that this was a very difficult place to work because if you did find a trap, there was no place to get out of sight and wait for the guy to fish it. He also pointed out the houses where the violators lived. I wrote their names in a notebook as he talked.

As we rounded a bend in the river, Bill said, "There's a white house just ahead where the worst violator on the river lives." When we drew even with the house, I saw a long pier running out from the shore. There were three people and a dog standing on the end of the pier. Bill said, "You can bet your life that there is a fish trap within a hundred yards of this place." I turned the boat so that we would pass close to the pier.

The men on the dock recognized Bill and pretended to be glad to see him. They inquired as to his health and a friendly conversation developed. The atmosphere was really cordial on the surface.

The dog looked as if it might be part rat terrier. It was small with black and white spots. It was also very excited about something. It was interrupting us with its barking, and the oldest man on the pier kept hushing and swatting at it.

We visited about the weather and about how low the water had dropped in the river the past few days. To listen to us, you would think that we all loved each other.

With all of the niceties said, I restarted the motor and we eased away from the pier. Just then, the little dog got absolutely frantic and jumped off the pier. You can imagine our shock when the pup didn't sink into the water. There it stood, on the surface of the river, barking its fool head off. Bill's mouth dropped open and I imagine that mine did, too. For some reason the guys on the dock looked more embarrassed than they did surprised.

A very brief investigation revealed that a big fish trap was sitting about three feet from the pier. The water level had dropped overnight and there were barely two inches of water over the top of the device. The dog was standing on it. Seeing that the trap was tied to the pier with a piece of binder twine, there wasn't much question about who owned it.

We lifted the trap and found a dozen white bass in it. I was surprised how candid the men were about it. They joined us in a good laugh over the dog's disclosure. They told us that they had just lifted the trap and the dog had been barking at the fish that were flopping in it. About then they heard our boat coming around the bend and quickly tossed the trap back into the water. The dark, turbid water of the Rock River hid the trap from us pretty well, but the little dog hadn't forgotten about it.

The oldest of the men finally asked Bill, "Well, are you going to give us a goddam ticket or aren't you?" Bill smiled and answered, "I can't give you a ticket, boys. I'm no longer a game warden. I retired two weeks ago." A big grin passed around the group as they began to think that they were going to get away with something. Then Laesch introduced me, the new warden replacing him. I wrote the ticket.

The Bark River winds down through the southeast part of Jefferson County. This stream was not nearly as dirty as the Rock River. It also ran colder and had a reasonable amount of dissolved oxygen in it. What all of this means is that fish will flourish here. There was a nice population of northern pike in the Bark.

Naturally, this meant that the fish spearers also flourished in the area. I snooped around the Bark very early the next spring. Northern pike run earlier than walleyes. As soon as I started to see a few fish moving upstream, I also started seeing rubber boot tracks along the banks. One evening I slipped up on a guy who was walking along the bank. He didn't carry a spear, but I stayed out of sight and followed anyway in case he was tending a trap or a net. He was checking all of the right places and clearly was interested in the fish run.

He rounded a little bend and disappeared from my view. When I came around the bend, I almost stepped on him. He was sitting on the bank, watching a couple big northerns wiggling their way across a shallow riffle. He was over 60 years old and had a bushy head of gray hair. There was a roll of fat around his middle that looked like an inner tube under his striped bib overalls. He saw my badge and said I was wasting my time following him around. He said he had got religion and gone straight.

He went on to tell me how Bill Laesch had caught him years ago spearing northerns. He said that he and a bunch of his buddies were drinking in a bar when someone came in and said that the fish were running and that there were almost a hundred right under the bridge down the road. The bar emptied and a dozen people went down to the river to look. The old-timer had a spear in his car and he took it down to the river with him. In just a few minutes, he had six fish up on the bank.

Soon others in the gang wanted to try it, and he passed the spear to a friend. The run was at its peak. The fish were easy prey. Eventually, everyone in the group had speared a fish or two and had them piled in the grass at the end of the bridge.

What he didn't know at the time was that Laesch was hidden in the woods 50 yards away watching through his binoculars. Bill could see what was going on, but it was too dark to identify the participants. He knew that if he tried to jump them, they would scatter and he would be lucky to get more than one or two. He crept up closer. Soon, he was standing behind a clump of brush just feet from the bridge. Still, it was too dark to identify the spearers.

It occurred to Laesch that it was probably also too dark for them to recognize him, and so he calmly walked into their midst. He went undetected as he moved from person to person, making positive identification of people he had known for several years. He made a mental note of each, but was interrupted when one of the group shouted, "Here comes a car." Someone else said, "Quick, hide under the bridge!" The whole crew hurried off the bridge, down the bank and huddled along the edge of the river. Bill Laesch huddled right along with them.

After the car had passed, everyone trooped back up on the bridge and recommenced the fun. By now, Bill had every one identified. He grabbed the one holding the spear and loudly announced his presence. He added, "Don't anybody move!" They scattered, flushing like a covey of quail, and Bill was left holding the man I was now talking to along the river bank.

It took most of the night to knock on all the doors and round up the rest of the bunch, but by daylight each and every person who had speared a fish had a ticket from sly Bill Laesch.

The old man told me that he wouldn't even have been down there with that big gang if he had not been drinking. If he had been sober, he would have quietly slipped away and gotten all the fish he needed without getting caught. He figured he either had to quit violating or quit drinking. He reckoned they were both troublesome, but drinking gave him the most pleasure, so he quit violating.

I asked him if those other folks still speared northerns. He said that most of them do. I told him I sure would appreciate it if he could give me some details about when and where. He said, "I didn't get that much religion."

***

Over the years, I ran into several reformed violators. They had usually had some experience which inspired their reformation and were anxious to share it. Some of them had a run-in with a game warden and some just had a run of bad luck.

One grown man told me that an old-time game warden had caught him with a spear and a couple of fish when he was 12 years old. The warden took his fish and his spear, admonished him to never violate again, turned the kid over his knee and gave him the only spanking that he ever got in his life. He never forgot it.

Many years ago, I had a visit with an elderly gentleman who was one of the few year-round residents on Phantom Lake in northcentral Wisconsin. He had moved to the little cabin on the lake sometime in the 1930s and had been there ever since. He looked as if he had once been a big man. Now he appeared to be in poor health and was a lot on the bony side. There was a gentleness about him and he could smile shyly and talk at the same time. According to him, there were a bunch of big largemouth bass in the lake, but he was having little luck catching them.

He said that, years ago, he had decided in desperation to become a set-liner. He knew that the law allowed only two lines and that they could not be left unattended, but he wanted some of those bass in the worst way.

He got a hold of a dozen one-gallon jugs, the kind that vinegar used to come in. He screwed the covers nice and tight on them and tied a piece of fish line about three feet long to the handy ring handle on each one. Then he tied a fishhook on the other end of the line and baited each with an active frog. He knew that bass loved frogs.

Just before sundown, he loaded all of the stuff in his boat and rowed around the lake, dropping a jug set off every hundred yards or so. But he noticed that they floated so high in the water that anybody passing the lake could easily see them. He went around retrieving them again, and he filled each only about three-fourths full of water and replaced the caps. Now they sat down nicely in the water and you'd have had to look twice to find them. Satisfied with his work, he rowed back to his dock and tied up the boat.

He went to bed that night reasonably sure that his set lines would not be found, and completely confident that, come morning, he'd have a mess of bass, some of which were bound to be dandies.

The guy spent almost two hours the next morning locating all of the jugs. They had drifted all over the lake. Some were back under fallen trees and a couple were stuck in a big weed bed near the middle of the lake. Eventually he had them all back in the boat, so he rowed back in and tied up at the dock. Every single frog had crawled up and sat on top of its jug all night and, of course, he hadn't caught a single bass.

Chapter 4

RED LIGHTS AND SIRENS

Folks say that this country is the world's most mobile society. I guess that's probably true. We have the most highways and the most automobiles. We also have the inclination to build more and more of both. Nearly everything we do begins with getting in the car. We go to work, we shop, we recreate, we procreate and we violate in, with or from our motor vehicles. This means that the game warden must also work from his vehicle most of the time. This makes some jobs easier and others a lot tougher.

One of the biggest vehicle-related problems that all law officers have is getting the suspect's automobile stopped so that he can talk to the guy. Most state's laws require an officer to have a "reasonable suspicion" that the occupant of a vehicle is breaking the law before the officer can make the stop. Is there something going on which would cause a reasonable person to suspect that the law is being broken? The officer doesn't have to be right. Upon investigation, he may find that, indeed, there is no violation. But the basis for his suspicion must be reasonable. If the court rules that the stop was not lawful, then it doesn't matter if a violation was uncovered or not — the guy walks. Even if he is an ax murderer, he walks if his arrest was the result of an unlawful vehicle stop. Most courts are sticking pretty closely to this standard today.

In northern Wisconsin 25 years ago, either the rule was somewhat less confining or people just felt that game wardens were always suspicious and rarely reasonable. It was then common practice to simply park our cars across the road in a hunting area and stop every vehicle that came along. It worked. If you stayed there long enough, you usually found a couple of cars with loaded guns in them, and sometimes some illegal game. I never lost a case in court because the judge ruled that the stop was unlawful. And I sure wasn't careful about the authority question.

Later, when civil rights activists reared their heads and our random roadblocks were questioned, a new system developed. Wardens would put a portable sign along the highway. The sign read: "Hunters checkpoint ahead one mile." There would always be a convenient side road a few hundred yards past the sign. Mobile hunters with a guilty conscience would quickly turn off at the side road. Of course, there would be no hunters checkpoint up the highway, but there would be a warden waiting on the side road, and he was sure to be reasonably suspicious of anyone who decided, at the last minute, to take that route. I'm not sure that would hold up in court today, either, but it worked at the time.

One of the more interesting vehicle stops I've seen was made on the main street of a small town called Webster, in northwest Wisconsin. It was 1962 and the warden in Webster was a rugged "French man" named Russell E. DeBrock. He was a former college boxer and he looked the part. Over six feet tall and weighing around 200 pounds, his reputation approached legendary status in those parts. He had an enforcement style that was uniquely his own. He ran the county the way he wanted and was almost never challenged.

I was stationed in the next county to the north and always enjoyed the occasions when he and I got together to work on a case. On this particular day we met in Webster to plan a combined effort on deer shiners near our common county lines.

We parked our cars on the main street and were walking across to DeBrock's favorite restaurant. There was an old Chevrolet rumbling down the street towards us. It became apparent that if we didn't step it up or if the Chevy didn't slow down, we were going to get run over. At the last minute Russ turned to face the car. It was driven by a shaggy-looking shifty-eyed character who looked as if he hadn't had a bath in a month. He decided not to run over Russ, and stopped.

Russ reached in the open window and took the keys out of the ignition. He walked to the rear of the car and opened the trunk. He pawed around in there, looking under old gunny sacks and newspapers. Then he let himself in the passenger side door and went through the interior of the car. He checked the glove compartment and under the seats. Finally, he tossed the keys back to the driver and walked away from the car, which still sat with the trunk and the doors open.

Although he hadn't said a word to the driver, nor had the driver spoken to him, it was obvious that the guy knew who Russ was, what he was doing, and didn't question his authority to do it.

When we sat down in the cafe, DeBrock said, "When you can't find a gun or any deer blood in that hoodlum's car, you have things pretty well under control." Legal stop? Naw. Did it work? Sure. Warden DeBrock didn't have what the law would call a reasonable suspicion, but he always seemed to have things under control.

He made a vehicle stop later that fall which would have passed today's rigid standard. Somebody with a new Buick Roadmaster was doing a lot of shining and shooting in the northeast part of Russ's area. Russ had made a real case study of the guy. He knew his name, where he worked, when he hunted, what fields he liked to shine and even what caliber rifle he used. In mid-October, Russ still hadn't caught this guy.

It was a Friday night, and DeBrock was supposed to be at a meeting in the courthouse. The meeting had been well publicized. Every outlaw in the county knew that the warden would be there. Many of them used occasions such as this to hunt. DeBrock was experienced enough to think right along with these people. He skipped the meeting, picked up the special warden that was working for him, and quietly drove to the northeast corner of the county.

Adjacent to a quiet little graveled road there was a five-ace clover field. Here, each night, several deer nipped at the season's last few red blossoms. This field was on the list of spots where the Buick frequently showed up. After hiding his car just off the road, Russ briefed his special on the operation.

The Buick would probably come down from the north at about ten p.m. It would drive out into the little field and shine with only the headlights. There would be two occupants in the car and, whether they killed a deer or not, it was likely that they would afterwards proceed south towards the place where the wardens would be waiting.

DeBrock planned to do a head-on block on the Buick. He instructed his special to hide in the ditch at the place where the stop should occur. If the passenger decided to jump out and run, he would run right into the arms of the special warden. Otherwise, the special should get in the Buick as quickly as possible and get hold of the gun.

Head-on blocks are like a game of chicken. The good guy's car and the bad guy's car are speeding towards each other. The red light and siren come on at the last minute. They end with the two cars sliding towards each other, brakes locked, hopefully, before they smash into each other. Specials hate head-on blocks, and this special had already ridden through a couple of these stops with DeBrock. The prospect of standing in the ditch and watching one was just fine with him.

The two wardens were standing in the road having a cup of coffee at a quarter past ten when a set of headlights appeared up the road. They stepped behind some bushes and watched as the car turned into the little field. The taillights were characteristically Buick. They could see two people in the front seat. The car drove to the rear of the field and the deer ran for cover. It was a moonlit night, and the deer didn't stand well for a light.

The car stopped. The lights went out. DeBrock speculated that the hunters would sit tight for a while and wait for the deer to return to the field. A cloud slid over the moon as the wardens finished their coffee. The field remained dark and quiet for nearly an hour.

When the car lights finally came back on, the Buick made a U-turn and started back out of the field. There didn't seem to be any deer in sight. DeBrock decided to stop the suspects even though they hadn't shot. It was illegal to shine deer with a gun in the car, and Russ couldn't believe the guy didn't have a gun along. It wasn't as good a case as he wanted on the guy, but it was getting late in the fall. This may have been the last chance he would get to look him over.

The special warden positioned himself in the ditch as Russ started the engine. DeBrock watched through the trees for the lights of the Buick. At what he hoped was the precise moment, he wheeled his car out onto the gravel and turned to face the oncoming Buick. The timing was almost too good. Eight tires plowed gravel. The simultaneous panic stops ended with the two front bumpers just inches apart.

The special jerked opened the passenger side door and dove into the front seat. He landed in the lap of a perfectly naked lady. She screamed.

This Buick was the wrong color. The driver wasn't the man they were looking for. He was a tavern owner with whom Russ was acquainted. The lady was not the tavern owner's wife, and it wasn't a deer that he had been trying to get back in that field. Although this had looked reasonably suspicious, it wasn't. This was extremely suspicious. Everything the wardens had seen prior to the stop was right by the script. They were legally justified in making the stop. Everything they saw after the stop ... oh, well.

Russ smiled and said good evening to the bar owner. The man tried to smile back, but his face wouldn't work. The lady held a small pillow over her face. They slowly drove away without objecting to what was, in all probability, their first head-on block.

Occasionally it happened that the suspects refused to stop their vehicles when ordered. Several interesting options were then available to the warden.

More often than not, the fleeing driver just wanted to get far enough ahead of the warden's car to get out of sight. Then he would throw the gun out the window. Usually, we just followed as closely as possible with our headlights on high beam so that we would see the toss. When the violators threw the gun, we wouldn't stop for it. We'd toss a hat or a glove in the road to mark the spot and continue the chase. If they threw the flashlight they shined with, we threw something else. When they tossed the ammo, we'd toss another marker. This could go on until both cars were empty or you were half naked. Most of us took to carrying markers for this purpose. I carried several small paper sacks of white lime in the car. When a chase started, my special would hold one out the window. If they threw the gun, he slammed a bag down on the road. With the gun out of the car, the shiners usually stopped. After you had the bad guys captured, you could return to your marker and look for the gun.

If a real automobile race developed, one could try to call ahead on the radio for another officer to set up a road block for you. This rarely worked back then because there were so few law officers in the north.

The most interesting option was the good old ram. Every young game warden looked forward to his first ram. You just weren't a real, hairy-chested warden until you had done it. This was best accomplished by following the target car until it was just entering a curve. If you bashed it in the rear, when its front tires were turned a little, it usually spun around and went in the ditch back-wards. If this sounds a little silly to you, consider this — we were driving our own cars at the time. The state furnished the red light, siren and radio and paid us six cents a mile. We supplied the car, gas and oil, tires, insurance and repairs. Sounds downright stupid now, doesn't it?

If an officer rams another car with his car today, he is considered to have used deadly force. The bad guy better have been doing something that warranted the application of such force. Shining deer probably doesn't cut it. (Things just aren't as much fun as they used to be.) I performed two ramming exercises in my zeal to prove myself as the genuine article. They were both disasters. They do, however, serve to illustrate how far a cult-driven ego can be pushed.

One night, I was sitting on the hood of my new 1961 Ford, just waiting for some sucker to shoot one of the deer in the field across the road. My supervisor was sitting next to me. I think he was evaluating my performance, or something like that. It had been a long, cold night and we were sick of it. A few minutes before we would have given up, a customer came along.

A nice new Dodge stopped on the road and the driver stuck a bright flashlight out the window. He looked the field over as well as he could. A clump of brush screened one end of the field from his view. Of course, the deer were feeding at that end and he failed to see them. He drove on. I slipped the Ford in behind him, without lights, of course, and we followed him for several miles.

We cursed our luck as the Dodge stopped at two more fields but kept coming up empty. We tailed him along the twisting, hilly road until we met another car. It was decision time. If we passed the other car, they would surely see us. There was no side road to duck into and let the oncoming car pass. We would have to stop the Dodge right there and see if the driver had a gun.

I turned on everything. The siren wailed, the red light flashed, and the Dodge split. If it had been a straight road, we probably would have lost. That Dodge could really fly. As it was, 70 mph was tops, as the road turns and dips to cross several little bridges over creeks which drain into Lake Superior.

Finally, going into a shallow turn, my boss hollered, "Hit him!" and braced his feet against my new dash. At last, I was about to join the fraternity.

After the crunch, both my headlights went out and the Dodge went even faster. Now I had to keep up. I was using his headlights, and losing the race meant plunging into darkness and probably the ditch.

I caught up and hit him a second time. The rear end of his car bounced up and swerved violently. We flew past a cloud of dust and some chrome chunks in the air. His trunk was now open and the bumper was sagging several degrees on one end. I was losing my enthusiasm for the game when at last he pulled over and gave up.

We ran up, clamped him in irons, and searched the car. There was no deer. There was also no gun. There was no evidence that there ever had been either. The driver was wearing a suit and tie. We didn't have a case. Oh, we could always have charged him with failure to stop for an emergency vehicle, but under the circumstances that sounded sort of shallow.

He told us that he was on his way home from working late. He had stopped for a beer and was just looking to see if there were any deer around. A week or so before, he had received a ticket for drunk driving, and he thought we were traffic officers. He didn't want to lose his driver's license.

We cut a deal. The boss suggested that if he kept his mouth shut and repaired his own car, we'd keep our mouths shut and not turn him over to the traffic cops. I guess great inspirations like this are what makes one a supervisor.

My boss and I sat alongside the road until it got light enough for me to drive home. I didn't like paying for the front-end work on my car, but what really ticked me off was it was such a good ram and I wasn't going to get any credit for it. By the time my next opportunity to ram came along, the state was buying the cars for us.

Superior is located at the western tip of Lake Superior. There is a large natural harbor there where lake freighters and ocean-going vessels dock. The north end of the city is a waterfront area criss-crossed by miles of railroad tracks. Train cars loaded with grain from the western states are pushed up and unloaded into huge elevators on the docks. Later the grain is dumped into the hulls of the big ships.

The train yards are covered with a dense weed growth. When the train cars are moved, a little grain shakes out of each one. The combination of dense cover and waste grain created perfect habitat for ring-necked pheasants. Normally, these birds do not survive the winters this far north, but the yards in the north end of Superior are teeming with them. There is a city ordinance prohibiting the use of a firearm in town, and so, even during the open season, the birds are protected.

There were, however, a bunch of people who just couldn't stand to see those delectable game birds loafing around in town and getting fat. They came up with several schemes for harvesting them. Little snares, made of monofilament fish line and set along their trails, were very effective. Some violators used steel leg-hold traps, normally used on mink or muskrat, and scattered corn around on the ground to bait the birds to the traps. The most ingenious system I knew of employed a two-foot length of six-inch-diameter stove pipe. One end of the chimney section would be plugged with a heavy screen. Then they put it flat on the ground and tossed a few kernels of corn into it. The pheasants crouched down and sneaked into the pipe for the corn, and, for some reason, they couldn't back out. There was fresh meat waiting when the clever violator returned.

I spent a lot of time in the winter trying to catch these guys. They all knew what my car looked like and there were few places to hide and wait for them to pick up their birds. Finally, the old retired warden living in Superior told me how to do it.

I got hold of some old denim clothes and a scotch cap, like all of the railroaders wore. Then I tied my pants cuffs around my ankles, like they did, put on a pair of chopper mitts and walked along the tracks carrying a broom. I would stop and sweep the snow out of the track switches as I had seen them do. This put me in the right

49

place while the violators were running their traps and I caught a few outfits that way. The word got around, however, and that no longer worked.

The solution appeared when I made friends with a nice guy who worked on top of one of those big grain elevators. While on the job, he overlooked much of the best pheasant cover. He liked the birds and scattered corn for them every morning. When someone messed with the ringnecks, he would give me a call with locations, descriptions, and so on. I no longer did routine patrol down there.

One winter day, I was just sitting down to lunch when the phone rang. It was him. Some brazen crooks were driving around by the grain elevator, shooting a shotgun out the windows at his pheasants. It was only three miles from my house and I was there in minutes.

Just west of the shipyards there was a large low area grown up in alder brush about 10 feet tall. There was a maze of little driving trails that meandered through the area. It was here that he had seen the outfit. I was particularly enthusiastic because the description he had given me over the phone matched the vehicle that Bob Jordan drove. Jordan was a well-known violator, and I had received several complaints about him. I had never caught him, however.

I began cruising the little lanes, watching for a late-model light-blue Chevrolet. The roads had not been plowed, the snow was hard packed and it was slippery going. It wasn't long before, approaching an intersection, I caught a glimpse of light blue through the alders to my left. I accelerated to get to the intersection ahead of the other car. I was plenty early. He was still 30 yards ahead of me when I rounded the corner towards him.

Besides the driver, there was one other occupant. He was in the center of the back seat and was feverishly active. Judging from the way the shotgun shells were flying up and hitting the inside of the car roof, I assumed he was unloading. I stepped on the gas to get up there and grab the man I now recognized as Jordan before he decided to run. To my surprise, the Chevy's driver also sped up and began easing over to his right. It looked as if he planned to get by me and run. I knew neither of us could stop, but I wasn't going to lose this outfit. I turned in front of the other car and there was a wonderful crash.

I was a little slow getting to their car because I had hit my nose on the steering wheel. I opened their back door and saw that Bob had gotten the gun back in its case. There was about half a box of shells rolling around on the floor. Several were fired empties, and I could smell burned powder in the car. I knew I had caught myself a bandit in the act. Now I had to find some hard evidence.

I went through that car with a fine-tooth comb. I even pried off the hubcaps and looked under the hood. I couldn't find a feather. If they had killed any pheasants, they had stashed them somewhere to pick them up later. This was starting to feel familiar. I had just had a head-on collision with a citizen on his side of the road. It had happened so quickly that I hadn't even had time to turn on the red light or siren. There was nothing I could bust them for.

The bumper of my patrol car had ridden up over his bumper, and my damage wasn't as bad as I had feared at first. Both front fenders, the grille and the hood of his car were wiped out. A large puddle of anti-freeze was growing larger, so his radiator was obviously broken, too. About then I noticed the kink in his roof. It ran from door post to door post across the top of the car. This was going to be expensive.

I asked them a lot of questions about what they were doing down there, where they had hidden the birds, if they realized how much trouble they were in and things like that. I didn't expect to get any answers from them. They didn't surprise me. They were plenty nervous and knew how close they had come, and they weren't saying a word.

I turned and walked back to my car. As I was getting in, Jordan asked, "What about my car?" I tried to act as if I made all of my stops that way and said, "What about it?" I got in and drove away. I didn't make out an accident report and I guess he didn't either.

To this day I have never heard another word about it. As I said earlier, folks just weren't suing each other over every little thing back then.

Chapter 5

BEARS, BEARS, BEARS

Hikers and backpackers will often strap noisy little bells to their ankles. The idea here is (and it's a pretty good idea) to make quite a bit of noise when you're wandering around in bear country. Most bears don't like being snuck up on. The bells announce the pending arrival of a human. If you wear hiker bells, the chances are good that you won't ever see a bear.

There are several differences between black bear and grizzly bear. The most important distinction is their disposition. The grizzly is just plain mean. He will attack a person with little provocation. Although there are only a few hundred of these ornery devils in the lower United States, there are several people who get chased, bitten or eaten by one of them every few years.

One day I was visiting with a tough old broad who ran a pack string of mules in Montana's Bob Marshall Wilderness. We were swapping experiences and opinions on bear. After I told her about several run-ins I'd had with black bear, she took off on grizzlies.

She'd been packing for years and she'd had her camps wrecked, her mules run off and the hell scared out of her by grizzlies. She said that she always sang as she rode the trails, figuring that the human voice should make it more clear than any tinkling bells would who was coming up the trail. She asked me if I had seen any grizzlies.

I told her that I hadn't seen any bears at all lately, but that I was seeing a few tracks and also some scats. I mentioned that I really didn't know how to tell grizzly scats from black bear scats.

She said, "The grizzly shit usually has hiker bells in it."

There are a lot of black bear in northern Wisconsin. After deer, they are probably our most highly prized trophy animal. The meat isn't particularly good, being a little coarse and too strong for most people's taste. They are much harder to skin than deer, and dragging the slain carcass out of the woods is almost more than one man can do. Yet, each year, thousands of would-be Daniel Boones mail in a permit application and hope that they are one of the lucky ones who receive a bear license. I think that the real attraction is the fame and notoriety that comes with being a successful bear hunter.

Bears are really interesting animals. Their eating habits closely resemble those of the pig. They will eat anything. Their usual diet includes fruits, berries, roots, insects and some small mammals. They get in a lot of trouble with people because they also like sweet corn, hogs, honey, sheep, garden plants and cattle. Their all-time favorite grocery is garbage.

If you follow a bear around for a while, you can tell exactly what it has been eating. They make frequent toilet stops — lots of little piles, not great big ones as you would expect. Whatever they've had to eat lately is there and it doesn't change appearance much. If they have been eating a farmer's corn, it shows in their scats. If they ate a sheep, the wool will be there.

The bee man fills those white boxes with little wooden squares that look like picture frames. There are strands of wire stretched back and forth across the frame to help the bees deposit their comb and store the honey. It's not just in nursery rhymes that bears like honey. They love the stuff and they really hog it down. Their scats will then be full of chunks of wood and tangled wire from the frames. Come to think about it, it might be an insult to say that they eat like pigs — an insult to the pigs, that is.

Bears' table manners are as much to blame for the damage they do as is the stuff they eat. If a bear takes a liking to sweet corn, it has a funny way of eating. It will roll around in the rows until it has about half an acre down flat and then it will start shoving down the ears of corn. Bears also do a lot of extra damage when they pick apples. After they've scarfed up all of the windfalls, they climb up in the tree to get at more. Bears are heavy and apple trees are fragile. You can tell an apple orchard that bears like from a long way off. They break a lot of good fruit-bearing limbs out of the trees.

The bear's strength is legendary. One can kill a full-grown cow in seconds. They do the same to pigs and sheep. They like to drag their kill off a ways before they eat, and they move an animal which weighs three times as much as they do with relative ease. They also have pretty good speed and can run down any animal that is slower than a horse. Black bears are easily capable of killing humans. Unlike the grizzly, they very rarely bother with us. Maybe we're the one thing that doesn't taste good to them. Bears are nocturnal by nature. They do most of their traveling and feeding after dark. I suppose they lie around and belch all day.

The Conservation Department used to have a program that paid folks for the damage done by bears. There were a lot of complicated forms to fill out, and then there was never enough money in the fund. Damages were prorated and paid at the end of the year. The claims usually paid about 50 cents on the dollar.

The bear damage program was administered by the wardens and, because there was never enough money to go around, we were always pressured by the farmers and the department to abate the damage as quickly as possible. We became hunters and trappers of bear. The big objection most of us had to it was that the damage usually started in the early fall when we were busy with illegal deer hunters and were already working twelve hours a day.

Sometimes we sat near the damage claim with a rifle, and when the bear returned to feed, we would kill it. This often ended the damage and then the claim was filled out. Shooting was a really time-consuming way to settle bear claims, however. Most of the guys preferred to use traps.

Each warden in bear country was issued one or two big leg-hold bear traps. They weighed over 25 pounds and you needed special clamps to compress the springs so that you could set the pan trigger. It was a little work making the set, but then you could leave and get some real work done. If a bear walked into the trap, he would be waiting for you when you returned the next day. The trapped bear were also shot.

Trapping means baiting, and sometimes it was hard to find something that the bear liked better than whatever he had already been eating to cause the damage. Different bears had different tastes, so there were no easy answers. It didn't always follow that they would rather eat strawberry shortcake than lima beans.

Warden Tony Jelich clued me in on a bait program that worked pretty well. Whenever he found a car-killed deer along the road, he would drag it back in the woods and cut each hind quarter loose from the body. Then he would mark its location on a map and let it lie. In late summer, when the bear complaints started piling up, he had a ready source of bait all lined up. Whenever he set a bear trap, he would take out his map, locate the nearest deer carcass and go retrieve one of the maggot-covered hams and bait his set. Most bears have a taste for rotting venison.

If a bear was already eating meat, such as some farmer's prize Angus steer, he may not come to festering venison. On sets for those bears I used to try to concoct a dessert-like bait for them. A mixture of rancid bacon grease, peanut butter and honey worked pretty well. I'd put it in a big glass jar and set it in the sun for a week or so. It developed an interesting odor that was strong, sweet and not too unpleasant. After it had ripened, I would smear it on several slices of stale bread and put it in one of those net-like onion sacks. It often worked on meat-eating bears.

One of my best friends had a kid named Mark. Mark was about ten years old and a swell kid. He used to pester me to let him ride along with me when I was working. He was good company, and once in a while I'd take him along. That was the case one day when I was going to see a farmer about a bear that had killed some sheep south of town.

At the farm, we found two dead sheep and a farmer who was mad. They were bear kills all right. One of them had been dragged off and covered with sticks and leaves. That's a pretty good sign that the bear might be back to dine on the carcass again.

I decided to set a trap and began building a crib. A crib is a funnel-shaped pile of logs wired together on the narrow end. The idea was to put the bait way up in the point of the funnel and set the trap about half-way in the crib from the open end. If you placed a stepping stick on each side of the trap, the old bear could hardly keep from stepping in the trap if he went in for the bait.

I told Mark to hang around the car while I went off and cut a bunch of logs and dead limbs. It was real hot and I worked up a sweat by the time I had cut and dragged about 10 poles to the trap site. I'd been gone quite a while. Mark had, in the meantime, dragged the big trap out of the trunk, along with the clamps and hand tools. He was a lot of help as I wired the crib together and finished the set.

When I was ready to place the bait, I was surprised to see that the jar was open and some of the bread was gone. Mark said that he had gotten hungry while I was back in the woods and decided to start in on our lunch. He'd made and ate a couple of sandwiches. I wasn't worried about the peanut butter or honey but I couldn't believe that the rancid grease was going to do him any good. I took another whiff of the stuff. It really had a strange smell now — a smell that didn't remind me of any of the ingredients.

There was plenty left to bait my set, so I did. I kept asking Mark how he felt and he kept saying, "Just fine." He felt bad about eating the bear bait, but I assured him that he hadn't hurt a thing. I did cancel our planned stop at his root beer stand on the way home.

I purposely waited until school was out the next day before checking the bear set. I knew Mark would get a kick out of seeing a trapped bear. When I got to the house, his mother told me that he hadn't gone to school that day. It seems that he didn't feel very good. He had a bellyache.

His eyes pleaded with me to not tell her about his bear bait lunch. I guess he figured she would put a stop to his traveling with me if she knew. When she left the room, he asked, "Can you imagine a bear eating a whole sackful of that crap?"

Usually, an adult bear weighs between 300 and 400 pounds. Before the days of the "sanitary landfill," bears used to take up residence at the town dump. These lucky bruins had access to all of the garbage they could handle. Some of these bears would fatten up to 600 pounds.

Dump bear were something else. They had big, saggy bellies that swung back and forth when they walked, and they almost never ran. They had so much aluminum foil wedged between their teeth that they looked as if they were wearing braces. They also stunk. You could trap one 15 miles from the dump but you knew it was a dump bear before you got within 50 feet of it.

People used to go out to the dump in the evening and watch the bears for entertainment. The bears got used to people standing around gawking at them, and the people got a little too used to the bears for their own good. I always wondered why nobody ever got scratched the way they used to pester the critters.

The bears could be sort of comical. One might come limping across the dump with an empty tomato can stuck on one foot and carrying a dead and rotting dog under its front leg. It almost seemed as if they were trying to make you laugh. In case you thought they weren't serious, you just had to stand around until one of them tried to take a particularly tasty prize away from another one. Brother, things could get pretty hectic in a hurry then.

Orchard operators in this state package cherries in big tin buckets that hold about four gallons. One night I saw a bear walking around at the dump with one of those buckets stuck on its head. I suppose it had jammed its nose down in it to lick out the last bit of syrup and found that it was a little too good a fit. He was pretty calm about his predicament and walked around slowly, banging into old refrigerators, barrels and other bears. Some nitwit gawker was figuring to go down there and remove it from the "poor animal's" head. Finally the bear reached up with one paw and pulled it off on the first try, just as if he knew he could have done it any time he wanted to.

One day a reporter from the local newspaper asked me to take him out to the dump to take some pictures of the bears. That evening, after supper, I picked him up. He filled the back seat of my car with camera cases, flashbulbs and film boxes and we set out. He was a friendly, talkative sort of character but clearly no outdoorsman. He wore thick glasses and was about 40 pounds overweight. A lot of that weight was packed in the big jowls that hung over his tightly buttoned collar. He still wore his wing-tip oxfords and the sport coat that he had on in the office earlier that day.

He mentioned several times that he was more than a little apprehensive about the assignment. I did my best to convince him that there was little danger. I suggested that he stay closer to the car than he did to the bears and he should be safe.

When we arrived, we were the only ones there except for seven or eight bears. We walked to within 50 feet of them and he started snapping pictures. When his first flashbulb went off, he quickly turned and started towards the car. He seemed surprised that the bears didn't chase him. After he discovered that the animals were only interested in eating garbage, he began inching up closer to them. Soon he was really into the project and shot several rolls of film. I began to get tired of it and walked back and sat on the hood of the car. He continued snapping pictures. After a while I heard him talking a blue streak and I realized that he didn't know I had left. I was about to holler at him and tell him I wasn't there. Then, in the dim light of the dump fires, I saw a big bear standing on its hind legs right next to him. The bear and the photographer looked about the same height and even had similar builds. The photographer was so preoccupied with his cameras that he thought that thing next to him was me. He was carrying on quite a one-sided conversation with the old sow. For its part, the bear just stood alongside him, watching the others digging in the garbage.

While I was trying to figure out some way to gently break it to my journalist friend that it wasn't me he was visiting with, he discovered it all by himself. He stopped talking in mid-sentence and stood there gaping in disbelief. It was several seconds before he moved a muscle, and then he moved them all at once. He lit out for the car a lot faster than I figured he was capable of moving. He jumped in, slammed and locked the door and said, "I guess that's enough for tonight."

***

Probably the best bear man in Wisconsin when I was stationed there was Cliff Freeman. He'd been the warden in Birchwood for many years and was one of those gentle giants. Cliff had been a wrestler in his younger days. Although he was almost 50 years old when I met him, he still had a heavily muscled frame and moved like a young athlete. His forearms and hands were huge, even for a man of his bulk. Freeman liked nearly everyone he met and often brooded a little after making an arrest. He just didn't enjoy making trouble for people.

Birchwood was pretty good bear country, and Cliff had a lot of run-ins with nuisance bears. He always trapped bears rather than shot them and had been at it long enough to have quite a reputation.

Cliff was also a pretty good amateur photographer and had a darkroom in his basement. Some of his photographic creations are still floating around many years after his death. He made several prints of a picture of a bear trap slammed shut on a man's boot. A leg bone with the shredded remains of a sock on it stuck out of the boot. It really turned your stomach when you first saw it. Then your mind got to wondering — did a bear eat the rest of him or was it wolves and crows that cleaned his bones? The truth is, it was one of Cliff's old boots, and he got the shin bone from a butcher shop. He got a kick out of the varying reactions that people had to the grisly scene.

Wisconsin wardens still talk about the time, more than 30 years ago, when Freeman set a trap on the back edge of an apple orchard that the bears were breaking up every night. The day after he made the set was his day off, and he was taking a drive in the family car.

Late in the afternoon, Cliff found himself within a mile or two of the orchard. He decided that he would go check his set. If he had caught a bear, he didn't want the thing to have to stand in the trap for a day and a half. It was a nice, sunny day and he was enjoying his stroll through the orchard. He munched on an apple as he approached the trap site. He was pleased to see that the trap had been sprung and had been dragged off into the nearby bushes. He peered over the top of the bushes and saw a yearling bear cowering at the end of the trap chain.

While he was walking back to the car to get a gun to dispatch the bear, it occurred to him that he was driving the family car and that there wasn't a gun in it. There was a big double-bitted ax in the trunk, though, and it was a small bear. He decided that he didn't want to drive all the way home for a gun. The ax would do just fine.

A few minutes later Cliff walked into the clump of bushes. The little bear turned to face him. With one fast swing of the heavy blade, Cliff hit the cub between the eyes. Instantly, its suffering was over.

Suddenly, there was a loud, deep-throated growl as a big sow bear, three times the size of the cub he had just killed, reared up out of the bushes a few feet away.

This turn of events had to at least put a lump in the throat of our best bear man. The sow lumbered a few steps towards him and dropped to all fours. She wasn't really charging, but she wasn't leaving either. She took a few more steps towards him until they were almost nose to nose. It was time to do something, and Cliff had few options. He started chopping. The sow didn't stand still as the trapped cub had. It took several swings and some fast foot-work to finish the job. I hear that Dan Boone killed a bear with a knife once. I don't think he ever got two in one day, though.

***

Lowell Swenson had a big bee yard in the woods across the road from his house. The bears really liked the honey that Lowell's bees made, and this situation was more than I could handle. I could expect my first call from Mr. Swenson shortly after the Fourth of July every year, and he would be livid.

The first time I ever saw the man, he hollered and scolded at me for 10 minutes before he showed me where his bee yard was. He held me personally responsible for the actions of every bear in the county.

The yard was a mess. A bear had tipped over four stacks of hives, and each stack was four boxes high. The boxes were smashed. All of the frames were broken and scattered, and what honey was left was not recoverable. Lowell said that there was over $500 in damage, and I didn't question his guess.

At the time, both of my traps were set on other complaints, so I would have to sit there with a rifle that night and hope that I could get a shot at the cussed thing.

I spent most of the afternoon rigging up my rifle the way a deer shiner I had caught recently had fixed his. I used a short piece of two-by-four lumber for a spacer and taped a bright flashlight to the underside of the barrel of the .30-06. When it got dark, I did a little test shooting. After a few shots and a couple adjustments, the gun was hitting right in the center of the spot the light made at a range of 25 yards. I went out and sat on a stump on the downwind side of Swenson's bee yard.

The mosquitoes were thick and it didn't take them long to locate me. I tried to swat at them with as little motion as possible. It started to rain. At first I welcomed this because it seemed to put a crimp in the mosquito swarm. Eventually, I was soaked and shivering and wasn't sure which of the two agonies was the worst. I thought about quitting, and then I remembered how mad old man Swenson was that morning and decided that I'd have to stay there all night even if the bear didn't come.

For once I got lucky. I had been there less than two hours when I saw a movement in the dark yard. I flipped on the flashlight. There were two red eyes reflecting back at me over the top of a stack of the white boxes. I tried to aim between the eyes, but I couldn't pick up the cross-hairs of the scope against the dark background. That bear wouldn't stay there long. I lowered the gun a bit until I could see the cross hairs against the white of the top box in the stack. It looked as if the bear was right behind the boxes, so I fired. The box exploded and the red eyes disappeared.

With a good deal of caution I sneaked up and found the bear lying dead. The bullet had gone through the box and hit it in the center of the chest. He fell forward on what was left of the colony of bees and did another $100 worth of damage on his way down.

Lowell must have been awake and heard the shot. He was standing alongside me within minutes. When he saw that carcass lying on those busted boxes, he started in on me all over again. I'll never forget the sight of him standing there with his bony white legs sticking out the bottom of his nightgown, swatting at bees and mosquitoes and cussing me for wrecking another colony.

Swenson's place was a jinx for me. I was far from the best trapper in the area, but bears aren't really that hard to trap. It seems as if I had a trap in his yard most of every fall. I could set on another claim and often have the troublemaker caught and killed the first night. I worked my can off for old Swenson, but for some reason I missed a lot of bears at his place.

One day I was having coffee with Mark's dad, Chuck Androsky. He operated an auto body shop in town. A deputy sheriff walked in and told me that he had heard the dispatcher on the radio trying to call me. I went out to the car and checked in. The dispatcher said that a bear had finally stepped in a trap at Swenson's. The old man was trying to find me.

I asked Chuck if he had ever shot a bear. He hadn't and he thought he'd like to give it a try, but he had to tow a car into town. We decided to combine the two trips, and that's why we pulled into Lowell Swenson's bee yard in a red wrecker that said "Superior Auto Body" on the door.

Chuck loaded the rifle and we began following the trail that the trap drag made through the woods. We noticed that a lot of small saplings were snapped right off. This was a big, strong bear. In about a hundred yards we caught up to him. He had circled around and was pretty close to Swenson's house. He must have lost his temper where the anchor stopped him. The ground was all torn up within the radius of the chain, and several small trees were chewed off level with the ground.

We startled the bear and he jumped straight up into the tree he was hooked on. He hung on about four feet above the ground. The big trap held him by two toes on his right front foot. He was the most athletic bear I'd ever seen. He had a large frame, but a lanky build. There was very little fat on him. He reminded me of a gorilla as he perched up there, glaring at us. Chuck fired once. I think the bear was dead before it hit the ground.

Old Swenson had followed us into the woods and, from a safe distance, had witnessed the execution. For once he had very little to say. He watched quietly as we dressed out the animal and Chuck drove his wrecker back to the spot. He used the winch on the wrecker boom to pick up the bear, and we drove back to town with the big black carcass swinging on the wrecker hook.

The next time a bear broke up Swenson's yard he called Chuck's body shop. Chuck told him he'd have to call the game warden and tell him about it. Lowell said, "To hell with the game warden. You're the one that kills bears. Get out of here!"

Things got so bad that when I'd kill a bear on another damage claim, I'd load it on the back of the car and drive by Swenson's house, hoping he'd see me and think I got it at his place. Once in a while I'd kill a bear there, but usually another one started hitting the yard within a week and the damage continued. Finally, Swenson telephoned my boss at the area headquarters and demanded that they fire me and transfer somebody up there who knew how to trap bears. The boss did the next best thing. He sent Cliff Freeman to Superior to check out my sets and see if he could help me.

Cliff stuck around for a couple days. He gave me some good pointers and showed me how to make hanging bait sets that didn't require a crib. I especially liked that because building the cribs was a lot of hard work.

I introduced Cliff to Lowell Swenson. Freeman took one look at Swenson's yard and told him the reason he had so much bear trouble was because his hives were set back in dense woods where bears were really comfortable. If Swenson didn't move the hives out of the woods and into the open, he would have bear problems as long as he lived. Lowell told us what he thought of smart aleck game wardens who tried to tell him how to farm honey.

I've been gone from Superior for 20 years, but the last I heard, Swenson's hives were still in the woods and the bear were still in his hives.

Chapter 6

THE SPECIALS

In Wisconsin — not all states have them — there are some dedicated, intelligent and talented men who have served as "Special Conservation Wardens." Some have made a very valuable contribution to this enforcement program. There are others who weren't much good, and I imagine this still holds true. Regardless of how they serve, the pay is poor, the hours are unreasonable, a great deal is expected of them and they will receive very little recognition.

Years ago, the local warden just looked around and offered the job to a likely looking candidate, or perhaps he put a friend on the payroll. Everyone from bartenders to bankers turned up in the right front seat of some warden's car and served a hitch or two as a "special."

Today specials are officially known as "limited term employees," which is usually shortened to LTE. Now they must be at least enrolled in, and preferably finished with, the state's standardized law-enforcement training. Little else has changed for these people over the last 30 years. Most wardens still refer to them as "my special." They are part-time assistant game wardens.

Because of budget limitations, these people rarely work more than three or four months a year. For most of them, this is a second job. They come from all walks of life. Undertakers, carpenters, typesetters, auto body men, wealthy businessmen, policemen, barbers and college students have all "specialed." Most of them do it to put a little pizzazz in their lives. Those who do it for the money must not need very much. Some do it to get the experience to help them become regular conservation wardens.

A good special is very hard to find. Anyone who has enough nerve and ambition to take on this job usually has a good job already. A poor special is easy to find. There seems to be an endless supply of people who are out of work and just dying to be game wardens. Most of them have no idea what the job is about, but they like the sound of the title and can't wait to get the badge and put a siren on their car. One of these can get you in a lot of trouble.

Exactly what they do depends on their abilities and on the whims of the wardens they work for. Each special belongs to one warden and this warden has supreme power over the special. Complete loyalty to that warden is the first requirement. A special has a lot to prove before he is trusted to work out of sight of his boss. No two wardens will use a special in just the same way. Some wardens want an errand boy or a good conversationalist who will make the long hours of waiting pass more quickly. Some want a good lawman.

I specialed for four years and will always have a warm spot in my heart for those people. I worked for some very good wardens and for a couple of knuckleheads. It was a great experience that I'll never forget. I also came away with the determination to never again accept any job that makes me an "assistant" anything.

In the 1960s, Harris Kolb was one of the youngest game wardens in the state. He looked two or three years younger than he was, and this didn't make his job any easier. He had two or three years on the force and had proven himself to be a very capable, if somewhat impulsive, warden. He was sort of a restless, hyperactive person and was always wound up tightly and ready to go.

He hired a special. The kid was a pulpwood logger and big enough to blot out the sun when he stood up. He was almost a head taller than Harris, and the son-of-a-gun was handsome enough to be one of those movie stars who could play the part of a rugged logger.

He wasn't an overly bright kid, but Harris said that he had enough common sense to get the job done. He must have had, too, because as the fall wore on, Kolb kept giving him tougher and more demanding jobs. He wasn't flashy, but he was dependable and loyal. His name was Kenny, but we all called him "Logger."

Logger became a specialist on those miserable "lay jobs." I don't know why we called them lay jobs, but what it consisted of was this: Anytime we found some untagged traps along the creek, or some set lines, or an illegal deer that looked as if someone would return for it, we kicked the special out with a sleeping bag and a portable radio. His job was to hide himself in some brush where he could see the violator tend his traps or his set lines or pick up his deer. When or if the outlaw showed up, the special radioed the news to the warden, who was sitting comfortably in his car, listening to a ball game and drinking coffee. The warden then swooped in and made the arrest. Some of those lay jobs lasted 15 or 20 hours.

Kenny the Logger had the patience of a disciple and even volunteered for the job. Harris made a lot of really good cases with his help. They hadn't gotten in any fights with any outlaws yet, but Kolb was pretty sure that if they did, this guy was going to be lots of help.

One night, Warden Kolb decided to treat his good helper to a night on the town. Not their own town, of course, but a bigger town in the next county. They went over to Hayward.

About every third building on the main street of Hayward sells spirits. Kolb and his logger were determined to have a drink in every one of them. These guys had been working for 50 straight days and nights and they had a lot to get out of their systems. Kolb tried to do all of the buying, but Logger would have none of that. They happily drank from bar to bar and, as the night wore on, they became better and better pals.

Things started to deteriorate a little when they got themselves discovered by two lonely maidens in one of those bars. It wasn't that there weren't enough women for them. Two and two was four back then, too. The trouble was, and often still is, that one of those women was a whole lot easier to look at than the other one.

The trouble started when the pretty one took a shine to Logger. For that matter, so did the ugly one, but I imagine nobody noticed. Regular, permanent Conservation Warden Harris Kolb wanted the pretty one, but loyal, dependable, patient, part-time special Logger Ken was getting all of the attention. This was not the way the game was played. Harris did his best to subtly remind his assistant who was boss. The big kid just grinned and kept on hugging and patting away on his new-found love.

Kolb then launched a bunch of "war stories" about what a brave and fearless game warden he was. He showed the women his badge and asked them if they wanted to see his squad car. The homely one wanted to. Logger grinned.

Kolb said he had to use the bathroom, and he ordered his special to come with him to the men's room. Inside, Logger heard a lofty speech about dedication and loyalty, and then he was instructed to move in on the homely woman and clear out of Kolb's way so that he could hustle the pretty one.

When they got back to the table, Logger put his arm around the pretty gal, gave her a kiss on the neck, and grinned. In the military, this is called insubordination. Harris had no choice. He fired logger on the spot. He took his badge away from him and left him sitting there with the women. Kolb went home.

I never heard how Logger got home, or when. I did hear Harris say that the toughest thing he ever had to do in his whole life was the following day, when he rehired Logger and gave him back his badge.

***

Wally Marcyan emigrated to northern Wisconsin from Chicago. The slower-paced life-style was to his liking and he took to the northwoods, heart and soul. His roots were apparent, however, because he couldn't shake the Windy City accent. He did auto body repair work in a garage alongside his home on the shores of Clam Lake. He also did a little bartending at two or three resorts in the area.

One or the other of these occupations led to him becoming acquainted with a few of Wisconsin's game wardens. He took a liking to the wardens. Liking wardens wasn't a popular pastime around Clam Lake back in the 1960s. Wally was big enough that he didn't pay much attention to what the neighbors thought was popular, however.

Whenever a warden dented or bent his car, it was usually Wally who took care of the repairs. The price was about half of what most shops charged. I suspect that the labor was free when he worked on our cars.

He was a good-hearted son-of-a-gun and usually had a smile on his face. He also liked a good time as much as anyone I ever met. This sometimes led him to consume a bit more alcohol than the situation called for.

One of those people who would give you the shirt off his back if he liked you, Wally gave away a good share of his income by throwing big beach parties behind his house. He was a good cook and he wanted everyone to have a good time, plenty to eat and plenty to drink. It came to pass that these beach parties were peopled mostly by game wardens. Such loyalty did not go unnoticed, and eventually, Wally was dubbed "The Fender-Bender" and was hired as a special by the warden in Burnett County.

Wally was totally dedicated to his boss. There were a lot of laws that he didn't understand and many things about the department that he never bothered to learn. However, when he was given a job to do, you could bet your paycheck that it was either going to get done or Big Wally was going to get all used up trying to do it.

When he and his boss, Russ, went to work, Wally always brought along a lunch big enough to keep two men alive for a week. I remember one night when I was working deer shiners along my south county line and visiting with Russ and Wally on the radio. They were about 15 miles south of me and were out there for the same reason I was. It was a really slow evening. Eventually we decided to meet in a gravel pit on the county line and have a bite to eat. I didn't have any lunch with me, but I was pretty sure Wally would come through.

When I got there, Fender-Bender already had a fire going. Russ asked him what he was fixing to make, and Wally said "chili." We both complained that even if he had all of the ingredients, we'd be there until daylight before it was ready. About then, our chef grinned and took a big plastic bag out of a cooler in the trunk. The odd shaped mass was about a gallon of frozen chili. He announced that "all we've got to do is melt it and we eat."

His smile vanished when he started cussing, having discovered that he had failed to bring a kettle in which to do the melting. In a few seconds, he came up with a solution. He went around to the back of the car and knocked off a hub cap. Then he pulled out the tail of the shirt he was wearing (and had probably worn the day before, too), wiped some of the dust and grease out of the wheel cover and tossed it in the fire. With a triumphant smile, he shook the contents of the plastic bag into the makeshift pot. Sure enough, it melted and turned into chili — so much chili that it completely filled the disc right to the rim. We gingerly scooped it out with our coffee cups and, at Wally's suggestion, dumped off the top half-inch to get rid of the grease and grit. Thankfully, it was dark. As I remember, though, it tasted good.

One afternoon, Wally and Russ were cruising some backroads in the northwest corner of the county when they met a carload of familiar faces, a notorious gang of outlaws from Minnesota that used to slip over the state line and do their violating in Wisconsin. They were archers and they specialized in deer. Encounters with this outfit usually got physical.

71

Russ pulled across the narrow road, blocking the oncoming car, and flipped on the red light. As the bandits stopped, the wardens heard a rifle shot less than a quarter of a mile to the east. This was early September. No hunting seasons were open. The wardens now had two situations that needed attention.

Russ told Wally to search the car of the outfit they had stopped and to keep the suspects there until he returned. He then drove to the east to investigate the shot they had heard. The bow hunters got out of their car and started smart-mouthing warden Wally. He ignored the lip and jerked open all four doors. He pulled the back seat loose and tossed it in the ditch. Then he reached into the trunk from the inside of the car and popped the trunk open. (Only a good body and fender man could pull this off so quickly.) He knocked all four wheel covers off and then opened the hood.

The outlaws' mouths fell open in disbelief as the Fender-Bender began a meticulous search of every part of their car. In a few moments they gathered their wits and began protesting loudly at the treatment they were receiving. The big man, with three days' growth of beard and the badge pinned crooked on his dirty plaid shirt, kept searching. Finally the boldest of the four said, "I don't see any reason why we should stay here and take this guy's shit any longer."

Big Wally picked him up by the shirt-front and said, "I can't see where you were breaking any law, and I don't see why you should have to wait any longer, either. But my boss said to keep you here until he came back, and by God, you'll be here when he gets back."

Russ found an innocent target shooter down the road and, after a very brief visit, he returned. The first four suspects were sitting quietly on the shoulder of the road. They looked straight ahead at the scowling giant who had assumed possession of their automobile. He wore work shoes with paint specks of a dozen colors on them. There was no belt in his overall pants and nothing about him resembled the neatly uniformed warden who was driving the squad car. There was, however, some intangible threat of authority and force about him. They had decided not to challenge that threat.

There was no violation so the outfit was turned loose. This was not a fruitless stop, however. This group of outlaws knew now what they could expect from the law in Burnett County. The occasion also served to illustrate the dedication expected from a good special.

Wally specialed for four or five years. Whenever a gang of wardens gathered to work, he was assigned to cook and feed the crew. The food was always great and he always got the dishes done in time to jump in the car when his boss went back into the field. An awful lot of wardens in northwestern Wisconsin had bellied up to his table.

Eventually, Wally fell on hard times. Russ was promoted and transferred out of the area. Wally lost his home and his shop in a divorce. He began drinking more when he was already doing enough drinking for two normal men. He ran up a lot of bills and his creditors were constantly after him.

One year a few days before Christmas, I got a phone call from him. It was the first I'd heard from him in many months. He wasn't the kind of guy to feel sorry for himself, so I knew that his tale of woe was on the level. He needed a job.

I talked to my friend Chuck Androsky, who owned the body shop in Superior. He agreed to give Wally a try. I was there when he showed up for work the first day. He had lost a lot of weight and had dark circles around his eyes. His old blond crew cut had grown down over his ears and was showing a lot of gray. Chuck gave him a $50 advance and told him he had a job as long as he showed up on time and did good work. Wally's hands trembled badly as he stuffed the bills in his empty wallet.

I checked on him a few days later. Chuck said that Wally was a good body man. He did good work and he did it fast. Chuck had four young sons who hung around the shop. Wally had taken a liking to them and had spent most of the $50 on Christmas presents for the kids. He already had an unpaid tab at the Shamrock Bar across the street, too. In short order he made a lot of friends in Superior. A woman who lived upstairs over the Shamrock invited him to move in with her. Her ex-husband came and went occasionally and even he liked Wally. Wally referred to him as his "husband-in-law."

The old Fender-Bender put on a few pounds and got some color back in his cheeks. He also paid off a couple of old bills, but it was too late for Wally. One day he disappeared, leaving as many new unpaid bills as he had liquidated. He went back down around Clam Lake somewhere and used up what was left of himself. He died in his late 40s — a sad, lonely derelict with a heart of gold. He had been a darned good special.

***

Then there was Geno Rich. He was just five feet five inches tall. A big man in a clever disguise. He carried a Beretta automatic for a service handgun. The Italian gun in his pocket was the source of many jokes, and he liked a good joke as much as he liked spaghetti. Geno was always in a good mood and was able to see humor in nearly everything. If he had an enemy in the world, I don't know who it was. When I get to thinking about the really nice people I know, his name comes to mind early.

During Geno's indoctrination, I told him about the violators who would try to run away from us and would then probably fight when they were caught. He told me that he could run pretty fast, and catching them would be no problem. He said he might have trouble fighting with someone he wasn't mad at, though. He asked for advice.

Geno had been a dynamite high school fullback. I told him that when he caught up to them, he should just lower a shoulder and run over them the way he ran over those linebackers in football. Then, when they got up, they probably wouldn't have any fight left in them.

It was more than a year before he had the opportunity to exercise that theory. While checking fishermen, Geno ran into a greedy Illinois resident who took off on a dead run. The runner's live box was out on the end of a long pier, and he had about five times as many northern pike in it as he was allowed. He planned to hurry out there and dump them into the lake, thereby disposing of the evidence.

This fisherman was a tall, lanky dude and could really pick 'em up and lay 'em down. Down the beach he went at top speed. Geno was on his tail and closing the gap. When the fish hog made the turn and started down the long dock, special game warden Rich put on his best burst of speed. The poor fisherman slid to a stop at the end of the dock at the same time that Geno reached top speed and lowered his shoulder. There was a sickening thud as the two bodies flew off the end of the dock and lit in eight feet of water, fully 15 feet off the end of the pier.

There was a lawsuit threatened and some moaning about broken ribs and whiplash as the two swam and waded to shore. When the defendant straightened up and saw that the warden who had captured him so easily was almost a foot shorter than he was, he decided to keep the whole thing to himself.

Geno was able to find enough dying or dead fish at the end of the dock to prove the guy was well over his limit. We took him to court.

Geno was a master carpenter with a good job. I don't know why he specialed. I guess he was just having fun.

***

Of all the specials, though, Skip took the cake. He'll probably be offended to appear on these pages along with the specials because he became one of the most respected and colorful warden supervisors in the department. But before that he was the first special I had in my rookie year. He worked for me for over three years before he became a permanent warden. We made a lot of good cases and had a lot of fun.

Like all of us, Skip was a product of his early environment. I don't know what else could have made him so tough.

Laurence Darcy Cloutier was raised in the north end of Superior. This is a tough neighborhood. He found it necessary to contribute to the support of his family at the tender age of 14. He shot pigeons off the roof of the grain elevators along the waterfront and learned early that the small, young ones were the best eating. He also learned to run like hell when the cops showed up.

By the time he was 16 he was a janitor in a whorehouse. Skip shoveled snow for the women in the winter and mowed the grass in the summer. In the spring and fall, he switched the storm windows and the screens back and forth. He ran when the cops showed up there, too. It wasn't that he was doing anything illegal, but he knew the women were. Maybe it was just force of habit.

This was a pretty good job, but he lost it when modern technology came up with combination windows and riding lawn mowers.

Later on, he took to sweeping grain. The term "sweeping grain" probably is not understood outside of the Superior city limits so I'd better explain it.

Superior is a port city. Grain from the western states arrives in rail cars and is then loaded onto big ships for delivery to ports east. Those loaded rail cars are all sealed, but after they have been hastily dumped, there is always some grain left in the corners of the cars. While they are sitting around waiting to go back west, an industrious young man can make a few bucks after dark. All he needs is a broom and a few gunny sacks.

The local feed mill was glad to buy the stuff for a little less than it paid the farmers. Of course, one had to remember to run like hell when the cops showed.

Skip met a railroad detective once who could also run like hell. Then Judge Claude Cooper convinced Skip to quit sweeping grain. It was just a few years later that Skip was bringing cases before Judge Cooper with me. Claude Cooper was a wise old man and he grew to like Skip.

By the time I ran into him, Skip had done a hitch in the U.S. Navy and was married. He was working on a coal dock. His job was to go down into the hold of those big ships that had just unloaded a cargo of coal and, with a scoop shovel, he would scrape the leftover coal out of the corners and crannies. Then he would shovel it into a heap so that the big power shovel could scoop out the last of the load. Some personnel director had dubbed this the "clean-up crew." The pay was pretty good, but when they were finished with a ship, their clothes and their skin were so uniformly black they seemed to be made of the same material. I don't know what the insides of their lungs looked like.

Skip was a fairly big man and looked rough as a rasp. Even then, though, there was an authoritative presence about him. As the years passed, this grew stronger. When I interviewed him for the job, I could see immediately that he was both smart and tough. That was a heck of a lot more than I had expected to get for $2 an hour. He would work an eight-hour shift at the coal dock, go home and scrub for an hour and then work anywhere from five to fifteen hours with me, depending on what we ran into. The only jacket he had was a thin nylon windbreaker, but he never seemed to get cold or tired, and he never complained.

He asked a lot of questions — smart questions about the law, the resources and department policy. He remembered everything. It was clear that the guy was going places. You could also tell that he had already been in some interesting places.

One night we caught a guy shining deer and were transporting him to the jail in Superior. Although he was a skilled violator and a capable outdoorsman who had been hard to catch, he was sort of a shy individual. He had very little to say, but when we were almost to town he asked, "Am I going to jail?" I replied that, yes, he was. After a long pause, he said. "I've never been in jail. I really don't know what to expect." Skip said, "Let's see, it's Thursday, isn't it? You can expect macaroni."

I used to store car-killed deer in a local locker plant until I had arranged sales for them. The owner had given me a key so that I could get in after hours, and I more or less had the run of the place.

One summer night I had a big doe that I wanted to get in the cooler before the meat started to spoil. Skip was with me when we dragged the carcass in the door. There was an overhead track attached to the ceiling. Beef and pork halves were hung up on the track on pulleys and wheeled in and out of the cooler. I picked up one of the heavy steel pulleys which had a meat hook attached to it. I sunk the hook in the doe's jawbone and told Skip to pick the deer up. Then, with a long pole that had a hook on the end, I reached up and set the pulley on the track five feet above our heads. When I pulled the hook out of the hole in the pulley bracket, I accidentally dislodged the big contraption from the rail. It also came loose from the doe's jawbone and the whole thing fell down. I ducked away and heard it hit something soft before it bounced to the floor. I looked at Skip and he was still holding the deer carcass up as high as he could, waiting for me to hook it to the track.

I got busy and did it right the second time. Skip let go of the carcass and turned around. Blood was streaming down his face. The hook and pulley weighed over five pounds and had hit him flush in the mouth. There was an ugly gash inside his lip and a front tooth was loose. He hadn't made a sound, nor even flinched. The average tough guy would have cussed up a storm and dropped the deer. This was no average tough guy.

My new special got in the habit of stopping by my house after his shift at the coal dock. He wouldn't come in because of the shiny black coating all over him. He'd stand on the steps and I'd tell him what time I was going to pick him up and where we were going to work that night. One day when he arrived, my wife was busy sewing some curtains for the kitchen. Her machine was acting up and the project wasn't going well at all.

78

She stopped at the door to say "Hi" to Skip and had the failed project in her hand. He glanced at it and said that he knew what was wrong with her sewing machine. She asked, "Can you fix it?" He replied that he sure could. She said, "Get in here."

He unsnapped his bib overalls and let them drop to the step. Then he took off his jacket, shirt, and boots. He was now clad only in his underwear, which was surprisingly white except for a black smudge at the fly of his shorts. He stepped in the door, went to the bathroom and washed his hands and face and then sat down at the sewing machine.

In a few minutes he had the thing pretty well disassembled. He fiddled, oiled and adjusted for a while and then put it all back together with practiced skill. Taking the curtains from her, he began running hems and attaching lace ruffles. He put folds and tucks in all the right places and worked so quickly that the job was finished in no time. Then he got up and stepped out the door and into his filthy clothes and said, "See you later," and left.

He'd been a parachute rigger in the navy and they had sent him to school to learn all about sewing machines. I'll never forget the sight of that big guy, sitting there in his underwear, making lace curtains.

One day I found a fish trap in the Nemaji River, near the state line. The walleyes were not running and there were only a couple of suckers in it. There were fresh man tracks where it was wired to a stump, so it was still being fished. This wasn't the best case in the world, but it was worth working.

I went to town and got a thermos of coffee and a sandwich. I told my wife I would probably be gone all night and headed out the door. There I met Skip, who had just got off work. He insisted on getting in on this because he had yet to help catch a fish trapper. He put a boat cushion on the seat of my car to protect it from the coal dust and jumped in. I told him he would have to wash up in the Nemaji River when we got there.

79

I hid my car on a woods road and we walked a half mile or so to the river. I rechecked the trap while Skip was rolling up his sleeves for a cold-water wash job. At that instant we heard a car door slam over near the road. There was a good chance that our trapper was already here. Skip's wash job would have to wait. I looked around for a spot where we could get out of sight to watch the trap.

The river cut through a big hill at this spot and the red clay banks were about 60 feet high and almost vertical. We were standing on a narrow trail that ran along the shore at the foot of the steep river bank. I guessed that if we laid flat on top of the bank, right above the trap, we would probably go unnoticed. We ran up the trail a ways to a spot where we could climb on top of the bank.

At the top of the bank there were three or four downed birch trees. One of them hung out over the bank. They were about six inches through the butt and maybe 20 feet long. We crawled in under them and inched forward until we could just peek down over the bank, directly above the fish trap.

Within five minutes, two men came walking along the narrow path from the road. The first one was gigantic. He wore jeans and a work shirt and had curly blond hair. The other was a little pot-bellied guy with dark hair. They were both about 30 years old. They talked in a normal tone of voice and were not at all wary or cautious. They walked directly to the trap, and the big blond guy pulled it up by the wire. He held it up and examined the contents. "Nothing but suckers," he said with contempt and tossed it back in the river.

I'd seen enough to charge him in court with operating a fish trap. I nodded at Skip and stood up. I took about four careful steps, each one about 15 feet long, down the steep bank, and found myself standing between the two violators. Before I could say a word, the little potbellied guy turned to run. I grabbed the collar of his coat and identified myself as the game warden. Hanging on to him, I turned towards the giant. He had an ugly, mad look on his face but was still too surprised to take any action. I told him to get his fishing license out for me. I didn't even care if he had a license. I just wanted to give him something to do besides breaking my neck.

He backed up a step or two and acted as if he might run. He was so mean looking that I almost wished he would. I grabbed his sleeve with my free hand and warned him not to try anything funny. I had no idea how I'd back that warning up if he didn't heed it.

By now it occurred to me that my special still hadn't arrived on the scene, and I sure could have used his help. I looked up the bank and saw that he was tangled up in the branches of one of those birch trees. He had to be a little careful because he was within an inch of falling head first down that bank. Finally, he threw caution to the wind and grabbed the trunk of the birch that stuck out over the bank. He kicked off with his feet and swung out below the trunk of the tree like a gorilla. About the time he intended to let go and drop to the bank, the birch tree broke off at the stump.

Special warden Skip Cloutier came racing down the bank, taking about 50 tiny steps a second and holding a 20-foot birch tree overhead. It must have weighed over 200 pounds. He slid to a stop on the narrow trail amidst our already crowded little group and, with a mighty heave, he lofted the tree over our heads and into the river. There was a hell of a splash that showered all four of us.

The fish trappers looked incredulously at the coal-black creature that had joined us. With a trembling voice, the biggest fish trapper I'd ever seen said, "Who in the devil are you?" Skip only scowled in reply. I said, "Uh, he's with me." He didn't look anything like any game warden they had ever seen, but it was apparent that he was on my side. That was enough. All thoughts of running or resisting left them. The giant handed me a fishing license. His name was Daytona and his physical description on the license read six feet five inches tall and 318 pounds. I don't know what I would have done with him if Skip hadn't been there and if the fish trapper had wanted to wrestle. Just taken my licking like a man, I guess.

When the meager funds I was allotted to pay a special were all spent, Skip refused to stay home. He said, "I'm your special. When you have money to pay me, that's good. When you don't have money to pay me, that's not as good. But I'm still your special." I don't know of any warden who ever had a better one.

Chapter 7

FEUDS AND RIVALRIES

By now it shouldn't surprise you to learn that there are rivalries between game wardens. Most often, the rivalries are friendly and productive and sometimes make for a lot of fun. Occasionally, they become more serious and develop into feuds. The feuds are rarely productive or friendly at the time, but they can make for some funny stories after things cool down.

Game warden feuds are usually turf-oriented and therefore are usually between neighboring wardens. Each warden is assigned a specific geographic area in which he is to concentrate his efforts. He is well aware of his boundaries and if he is good, he takes pride in keeping his area clean. He also isn't happy if another warden starts mucking around in there.

Under the new organizational structure of the department, new wardens are less territorial than we used to be. It seems to me that today there are more friendly rivalries and fewer of those knock-down battles. That's good, I suppose, but the old feuds are more fun to talk about.

When Randy Morse completed his training, he was stationed in the northwest area. Like most young wardens, he was full of enthusiasm and was anxious to establish himself as one of the good ones. He was doing a pretty good job of it, too. He worked long hours and was cutting a wide swath. Wednesday was court day, and Randy was usually there with two or three tickets. Things were going pretty well for the new kid.

There was another warden stationed in the eastern half of the county. Randy's neighbor was Conrad Cox. Conrad had been there for about 10 years. Cox had a well-rounded program and took his job very seriously. He worked hard and he made his share of good cases, too.

About the only time these two saw each other was on Wednesdays. Although they seemed to like each other, a rivalry began to develop. Conrad was sort of a practical joker and it was a normal thing to initiate a new guy into the group with a practical joke. He did a grand job on Randy.

Warden Cox knew Judge Donley pretty well. I don't mean that they were buddies, but Cox had been bringing cases to him for 10 years and he had a pretty good idea of how the judge thought on matters concerning fish and game laws. Donley, in turn, had a lot of respect for Cox as a lawman.

Like most judges, this guy was a little on the egotistical side. He was king of his domain — the courtroom — and demanded respect from all of the officers and attorneys who worked in his court. The officers were aware of this, and whenever they thought they might have gotten the short end of a case in his court, they quietly accepted it. There was no point in fighting the man who made the rules and the rulings.

One Wednesday afternoon, after all of their cases had been heard, Cox invited Randy to have a cup of coffee with him. Halfway through the second cup, Cox asked Morse, "Have you ever noticed what puny little fines that damned judge gives to deer shiners?" The two wardens talked this over for about 20 minutes, and Morse became convinced that Cox was right, this judge was soft on deer shiners. Conrad said that he and the judge didn't get along very well, otherwise he would have had a talk with him before this. Cox suggested that Randy was the one to go jack up the old boy about the meager penalties he was giving game violators.

All young wardens want to get along with and be respected by the old-timers. Randy saw this as an opportunity to make his mark with Cox. He also felt that he was getting along pretty well with the old judge and agreed that he was the man for the job. Conrad's last advice to the rookie was, "Be firm and don't take 'no' for an answer." Morse called the judge and made an appointment to see him in his chambers after court.

To make a long story short, when Randy was done reading that old judge the riot act about his little fines, being firm about it, and trying not to take 'no' for an answer, the old man blew a gasket. Donley's purple lips trembled as he told Morse in no uncertain terms who was running that court and what snot-nosed young game wardens could do about it if they didn't like it. From there on, it was all downhill between those two.

The judge got into the habit of dismissing any case that Randy brought in unless it was rock solid. Those fines (which really were about average for the times) that were too small before got smaller if Randy Morse had signed the complaint. This, of course, made Randy sore. He began publicly criticizing the court, and the two men were no longer on speaking terms.

The whole thing had gone a lot further than Cox had planned. It was now well known among all of the wardens in the area that Randy and his judge were at war. The supervisor got on Randy about the poor relationship that he had with his court and told him to patch things up. Nothing doing. Morse was determined to stand his ground and the battle raged on for months.

Finally, Randy decided that he was in a no-win situation. He had to take his cases to that judge, and things weren't going to change unless Randy changed them. He swallowed a big dose of pride and went in and made a long apology to the old man. He told the judge how he had let his enthusiasm for his work get the best of him. He said that he appreciated the guidance that the court was giving him, and he sure did want to patch things up. He almost gagged on his words as the old man sat there gloating. Finally, the two shook hands. Randy left feeling like a whipped pup, but hoping that the supervisor would get off his back and that his cases would go through court as they used to.

Morse told Conrad Cox, the supervisor and everyone who would listen to him that the judge and he had buried the hatchet. He had a bad taste in his mouth and it almost broke his face to smile at the judge, but things were turning out a lot better on Wednesdays.

Randy Morse liked to hunt ducks. His busy schedule didn't allow for much of it except for once in a while, when he could sneak away for a few minutes. He would jump a few mallards off from a favorite pothole near the county line. Cox had joined him on one of these outings and they had each shot their limit.

One day in October, Conrad was patrolling near the county line and he came upon Morse's car. It was parked alongside a narrow dirt road that passed within a hundred yards of the mallard hole. Randy was hunting. Cox eased his car over as far as he could and barely squeezed past his neighboring warden's car. He started to drive on when an evil impulse overcame him. The perfect practical joke had just come to mind with no effort whatsoever.

He took a scrap of paper and wrote a brief message on it and stuck it under the windshield wiper of the young warden's car and drove away. Within 20 minutes, Randy arrived back at his car. He saw the note and was surprised. The road was not well traveled and he had been gone less than half an hour. He took off his hip boots and put them in the trunk, along with his shotgun. He unlocked his door and grabbed the note just before sitting behind the wheel. He quickly read the short message and immediately flew into a rage. He started the car and took off for town as fast as he dared to drive. Someone was going to get a piece of his mind.

The note said, "Warden, If you'd learn how to park your damned car maybe a person could drive by on this public road. Why are you hunting ducks when you're supposed to be working anyway?" It was signed, "Judge Donley."

The rekindled battle raged on for as long as Randy was stationed in the county.

***

I didn't get along with my neighboring warden. He'd been stationed there forever and had no respect for the invisible line that was supposed to separate our work areas. He was a good woodsman and knew every inch of his area like the back of his hand. He was also pretty familiar with most of mine.

Superior was the largest city for several miles and it was my assigned residence. Most of the action was there. The courthouse, the newspaper and the sheriff's office were all in the city.

A good field warden in northern Wisconsin creates quite a bit of news, and Ted was a good field warden. He also had connections with a reporter on the newspaper in Superior and they saw to it that he got plenty of ink. Ted had a regular game warden-sized ego and didn't like the idea of a new recruit moving in next door.

When I started, it became apparent that he had done a lot of groundwork in advance of my arrival. At least once a day, some hunter or fisherman would size me up and say, "So you're the new helper they hired for Ted." This didn't sit well with me. I was a regular warden, just as he was, and I was working on an ego just as big as his. I'd usually answer by asking, "Who's Ted?"

He'd schedule a speech before the Sportsmen's Club in my hometown and I wouldn't know a thing about it until I read it in the newspaper the next day. This was a pretty serious breach of game warden etiquette.

The next day, I'd go over and check boaters on the lake nearest to his house until I found some poor soul who didn't have a life preserver in his boat. I'd tell him that if he'd go buy a preserver and drive over to my assistant's (Ted) house and show it to him, I wouldn't give him a ticket. Then I'd lie awake half the night giggling at my vision of Ted's face when that guy told him about me working on his lake.

This silly stuff went on until we had both worked up a good hate for each other. What we had now was a good old-fashioned feud, and I didn't intend to be the loser. Neither did Ted. I suppose it drove our supervisor nearly nuts. He was always refereeing some trivial dispute that he had heard about through the grapevine.

This thing reached the point where we weren't speaking to each other. This is unhealthy because, once in a while, neighbors need one another. One night, I was working over his way and I heard him call on the radio for anybody who could give him a hand with an outfit that he was trying to stop. I took off right away. I don't know today if it was because of the brotherhood of wardens that I was rushing to his aid, or because I was going to get a kick out of stopping a crew that he couldn't get stopped. It doesn't matter, because when I got there, he had them stopped and they were in handcuffs. I asked if there was anything I could help him with. He didn't even turn his head towards me nor acknowledge my presence in any way. I left. We probably should both have been given a month off without pay about that time.

Along our disputed border, there was a section of state highway that had been recently rebuilt by the Highway Commission. As was usually the case on new highway jobs, the deer were feeding on the new seeding along the shoulders of the road. Naturally, the deer shiners knew about it and were working it pretty hard.

In this part of the county, my area and Ted's area overlapped. We both worked it. It became known as the "demilitarized zone," or the DMZ. We both had territorial rights there and couldn't argue about it.

When working deer shiners, it's very often difficult to find a place to hide your car so that you won't be found. That was the case on this choice piece of shiner habitat. At first, I used to park behind a shed on the west end and follow the likely looking suspects east with my headlights off. This worked, but it wasn't ideal. One afternoon I found a perfect spot to put the car out of sight, right in the middle of the stretch of highway. There was an old abandoned gravel pit back from the road about a hundred yards. It hadn't been used in years and the entrance was all overgrown with brush and small trees. I could drive down through the grassy ditch, between two aspen trees, and back into the pit. Then I'd brush my tire tracks off from the shoulder of the road and stand the grass up as best I could.

This spot was so good I had trouble finding it myself. In order to locate it at night, I drove east to a certain mailbox, past 31 telephone poles, count seven dashes in the highway center line and turn hard right. It scared the heck out of anyone who might be riding with me because it looked as though we were going to crash into the woods.

I used to refer to the place as "the cut," and, of course, I never told anyone where it was. From that spot I could look four miles each way and had a view of the complete deer area. I caught a good shining outfit the first night I sat there. I spent one or two nights a week there and it was amazing how they kept coming. I had the best fall I'd ever had on deer shiners, and over half of them came off from that little stretch of road.

All the wardens in the area knew I had a spot I called "the cut" and that it was a real glory hole. None of them knew exactly where it was, nor did they care. None of them, except Ted. He knew the country better than I did and it was killing him that I had one up on him here.

Late one fall, I was driving east, heading out to work deer shiners. It was about midnight. I neared my favorite spot and began counting dashes in the center line and was ready to turn into the exit. Suddenly, I was shocked to see an "X" painted with aluminum paint, right at the end of the seventh dash. This was how Ted marked his parking spots. I knew he had found my secret. I was just sick about it.

The next morning I gathered up a few materials and drove the 20 miles to where the "X" was on the road. It took nearly 30 minutes and half a gallon of turpentine, but I was able to remove all traces of the mark. Then I went east up the road about a hundred yards and painted one just exactly like it, opposite a little gap in the trees. Instead of a nice, level gravel pit beyond this gap, there were several low stumps and some big boulders.

I worked out of the cut every night for two weeks, waiting for the big event. One night a carload of drunks stopped and shot a deer right in front of me, and the score jumped another notch for the cut.

Finally, it happened. About ten o'clock one night a car came out of the west about 50 miles per hour. A hundred yards north of the cut the driver switched off the headlights and cramped the steering wheel to the right. There was a screech of tires as the sedan veered off into the woods. A wonderful crunch echoed through the night as Ted wiped out the front end of his car on one of the big boulders. I eased out of the cut and drove home.

We battled on for years, and I suppose the score was about even as we seemed to take turns jabbing each other. I never passed on a turn and I don't remember that he did either.

The day he finally broke the silence I couldn't have been more surprised. He asked me to meet him for lunch to talk things over. We should have done it in Geneva, but we met at the Coffee Cup Cafe. It was an uncomfortable lunch. Afterwards he started to talk.

He spoke in a soft voice about all of the frustration he was feeling, and as best he could, he apologized for his part in the battle. He recalled many of the dirty tricks we had pulled on each other, and although I get a laugh out of recalling them now, there was no humor in it that day.

He ended by saying that he was personally calling off the feud. He said that I could count on him for support in the future, if I wanted to. We shook hands and he left.

For a while, I figured this was another scheme and that something would come down on my head any day. As time went on, it appeared that he had meant everything he said. To this day he has never gone back on his word. We never did become fast friends, but we developed a good working relationship. I guess he won the last round. He was the one finally who was man enough to call it off.

***

This "turf jealousy" was quite common among wardens throughout the northwestern part of the state. George Latvilla told all of his neighboring wardens that when they crossed the line into Connolly County they had to whistle into their microphone so that he knew his space had been invaded. This, of course, had hilarious results. Any time any of us were within radio range of his area, we were whistling on the radio, but wouldn't respond to his calls to identify ourselves. We had visions of him chasing up and down his boundaries trying to locate the intruder who wasn't there. This situation was fun and it was funny. I think George enjoyed the joke too. He was a good warden.

Maybe there was something special about Connolly County. By far, the most possessive and territorial warden I ever heard of served there back in the 1920s. There are more legends, yarns and probably lies circulating about this man than any other who ever wore the badge.

Jack Lang was long gone when I went to work. Although there were two complete generations of wardens between us, his name still echoed through the legends kept alive by the old-timers of that time. All that I know of him was told to me by men who were just starting out on the force when he was working his last few years. I have no idea how accurate these stories are, but one thing is sure — he must have been quite a man. Somewhere between a tyrant and a hero, I'd think.

Ben Waters was transferred north to be Jack Lang's neighboring warden. Ben had worked in the Fox River Valley in the eastcentral part of the state and he was a tough hombre in his own right. Ben told me that he had met Jack the first night that he worked at his new station.

Ben set out to catch a deer shining outfit that he had received an anonymous call about. He drove out well after dark and found a spot to hide his car. Then he climbed a little hill that overlooked the area and sat on a stump. He had been there but a few minutes when the cold muzzle of a Winchester 30-30 was pressed against his neck. The soft voice of Jack Lang asked, "Who in hell are you?"

Ben had told no one where he was going to work and he hadn't heard a sound before the rifle touched him. It's probable that Lang originated the phone tip. That was an odd way to introduce oneself but, strangely enough, the men did become friends. The alliance was probably based on a lot of mutual respect.

According to all accounts, Lang was only an average-sized man. Apparently, he was handsome and had a flair for the dramatic. He was never seen without the 30-30. He always appeared well groomed and wore western style clothing. If uniforms had been issued back then, it's improbable that he would have worn them. Another old-timer told me that Lang would slide out of a sleeping bag after a night in the woods and there would not be a wrinkle in his clothes nor a hair out of place.

His influence in the county extended far beyond his duties as a game warden. Citizens were used to calling Jack with their problems rather than the sheriff. His endorsement assured the election of several county officials including the district attorney and the justice of the peace. His ability to nearly handpick these positions made him very powerful, and he knew how to use that power.

To many he was a Robin Hood-type character. It was said that he provided venison free of charge to several poor families and widows. Although the statutes provide for the sale of illegal game, Lang circumvented the paperwork involved with such transactions and used the meat to elevate his status with the natives. It was also implied that some of the illegal game may have been bagged with Jack Lang's Winchester.

About this time, fur was worth a lot of money, and trapping was a pretty lucrative pastime. Stories about "dollar-an-inch" beaver are true. The big beaver pelts brought over $80 each, and that was two months' wages for most men at the time. Of course, this situation put a lot of trappers in the woods.

Trappers are a lot of work for game wardens. Because they set their steel and leave for a complete day or two, apprehending them always involves long hours of waiting. With Lang's reputation, I can't imagine that there were many trappers who wanted to cross his path. Those who did have the nerve to break the law and take extra beaver were handled rather roughly by Lang. The first offense brought a trip to the justice of the peace and a stern warning that this behavior would not be tolerated in the future. If the trapper repeated the offense, Lang would set fire to the trapper's shack and burn it to the ground. Warden Jack Lang ran the county with an iron hand.

There was a woman working in the dry goods store and Jack took a shine to her. I suppose he was a pretty good catch, being both good looking and an authority figure. The romance was carried on rather quietly, as that was Jack's way of doing things. The fact that he was married may also have had something to do with it, although I can't imagine that he was afraid of his wife. At any rate, few people knew of the affair.

The woman was the only employee of a penny-pinching old proprietor. She clerked in the store for a pittance and the prospects of bettering her financial status were nil.

In a move to raise money for some badly needed municipal improvements, the village was selling tax-free bonds. The interest rate was attractive and the investment completely safe. The problem was that few people had enough extra money lying around to take advantage of the opportunity.

The dry goods storekeeper scraped together every cent he could and took his considerable funds to the bank to buy as many of the bonds as possible. Here he found out that the city fathers had placed a limit on the number of bonds that any one person could acquire. He had twice as much money as they would let him invest. He made his purchase and went back to the store where he brooded over his lost opportunity.

Late that afternoon he watched Jack Lang's girlfriend wait on a customer, and a thought occurred to him. He was sure he could trust the honest, hard-working clerk. He gave her the balance of his money and instructed her to go to the bank and buy a share of the short-term bonds in her name and bring them back to him. He swore her to secrecy concerning the matter.

For years she kept her word and, in fact, almost forgot about her name on the valuable certificates. She was reminded one day when her boss told her that the maturity date was very near and that soon he would be asking her to cash them for him. That night, she had a date with Jack Lang.

During the course of the evening, she told Jack the whole truth about the bond caper she had pulled for her frugal employer. Now Jack didn't like people doing shady things in his area. He also liked the woman a lot more than he liked the storekeeper, and his Robin Hood instinct led him to believe that the woman needed the money a lot more than the merchant did. He gave her some instructions of his own.

The following day, the clerk marched into the store and demanded that her bonds be turned over to her. Of course, her demand was refused. She threatened to go to the authorities about the scheme if she didn't get the bonds pronto. Perhaps he thought that she wouldn't make good her threat, or maybe he was scared silly, but her employer wasn't about to hand over that much of his life's savings. She stomped out the door, empty handed.

Within a few hours, the "authorities" arrived at the store wearing western clothes without a wrinkle and carrying a 30-30 Winchester. Lang told the merchant that he knew all about the fraudulent bonds and that he intended to seize them in the name of the law. Again, the old man declined to release the packet. No amount of arguments or threats could convince the old tightwad to open the safe and give them up. In desperation, Lang gave him 24 hours to produce the bonds or Lang would take "drastic measures."

Several hours later, in the middle of the night, there was a great explosion as half a case of dynamite went off. The entire front end of the dry-goods store was blasted out into the street.

Well within the 24-hour limit, the bonds were deposited in the clerk's mailbox.

If Jack Lang had asked me to whistle when I crossed his area line, I would have done it.

Chapter 8

NOBODY'S PERFECT

Her phone rang as I walked past her desk. Joanne was a new receptionist in the district office. She was a pretty blond woman with a good attitude about her work, but she had no previous experience that prepared her for dealing with the public on the telephone. Of course, she was also not yet aware of the department's policies, but she was trying.

I was almost to the door when she called to me. The caller she had on the line had a question and she wanted to hit me up for the answer as long as I was nearby. I was on my way to the airport and was a little late, but I stopped and listened.

A housewife was calling. According to her, a great blue heron had flown into an electric power line in front of the caller's house and had broken a wing. It had been walking around in the lady's yard, looking miserable, and so she had caught it and moved it to her basement. Now she was worried that she might be breaking some law. Her question was, "What do I do now?"

From experience, I knew that the chances of repairing the wing so that the heron could lead a normal life in the wild were about nil. I knew several "bunny huggers" who would take the poor thing and mother the devil out of it and it would spend the rest of its life pacing in a cage. They would then feel that they had performed a heroic rescue. I've always had problems with whatever drives those people. I've also always had problems with wild animals pacing up and down in cages. I think that wild critters like it best in the wild and that making captives of them is torturous. Whenever I ran into deals like this one, I killed the poor thing.

Joanne sat with her hand over the mouthpiece of the phone and that pretty smile on her face, waiting for my answer. I said, "Bat it in the head and toss it in the garbage." That was the quickest way to say it, and after all, I was in a hurry. I knew that she would shine that up and spice it with sympathetic niceties before she relayed it to the caller. I turned and headed out the door. I heard her repeat to the caller, "Bat it in the head and throw...," and then the door slammed behind me.

I stopped dead in my tracks, shocked. I jerked open the door and looked in to see her hang up the phone. "Thanks for your help," she said, flashing another pretty smile. I left.

That was dumb of me. I should have realized that Joanne would take me literally. (My supervisor had been telling me for years that I'm too flippant.) The caller picked up her phone again. This time she called the governor's office. I guess that was about as much hot water as I'd ever been in, and it was over an insignificant thing like a heron with a broken wing. Politicians don't care if every heron in the world drops dead tomorrow. I learned that they do care very much if some crude game warden offends one of their constituents. What the hell — nobody's perfect.

When Art Gillette was a kid, he idolized Billy Ness. Billy was two years older and a head taller than Art. In his mid-teens, Billy Ness had his own rifle, a little pocket money and a pinto pony that he rode everywhere he went. His folks didn't keep a very tight rein on him and he had a lot of independence. Art, on the other hand, had an old bicycle that was often broken and a lot of chores to do.

Billy was quite a hunter. He had a squirrel tail tied to the pony's bridle and several grouse feathers tucked in his hat band — trophies that attested to his marksmanship. Art would sit awestruck for hours, listening to the older boy's exploits.

Occasionally, the two boys stole away to the creek that ran behind the Ness barn. Here Art learned how to smoke cigarettes and found out that it wasn't the stork that brought babies after all. Billy showed Art where the walleyes spawned in the spring and taught him how to catch suckers with his bare hands. It seemed as if Billy was everything that Art wanted to be.

Billy got around to thinking he should try a little deer shining. He'd heard his old man and his uncles talk about how much fun it was. Fun, that is, unless the game warden caught you. Shining deer was the most serious violation in the game laws. But heck, he'd heard his uncles tell about the times they'd tricked the game warden. He guessed that he could, too. He kicked all of this around in his mind for a while and finally started making serious plans.

Naturally, he had to brag to Art about what a great adventure he was fixing to have. Art was just bursting with excitement over the caper and, although it scared him to death to think of it, he invited himself along. Billy thought it over and decided that the kid could be a little help and so he consented.

Over the next few days they did a bit of practicing and scheming. There was some equipment that Billy had to round up. Art's biggest problem was finding a good reason to be out of the house that late at night.

There were a few deer feeding on the fields at night, but they were pretty jumpy. Billy's dad and his uncles probably had something to do with the nervous state of the deer around there. The boys, however, came up with a pretty decent plan.

On the big night they sneaked over to an uncle's house and "borrowed" a canoe. They were going to drift down the creek that ran through a dense cedar swamp and then flowed through the Ness barnyard. The chances of seeing a deer watering at the creek on the two-mile drift were pretty good.

They were surprised how dark it was after they got the canoe in the water and pushed off. There was no moon. A heavy overcast completely blocked the starlight. Billy sat on the front seat with his .22 rifle propped in the bow. He held the big flashlight in both hands. Art sat in the stern and used a long push-pole to help keep the craft moving quietly downstream.

They had planned to use the light sparingly to avoid detection. The trouble was that every time Billy turned off the light, Art couldn't see a thing. It was as though someone had pulled a black bag over his head. Every few seconds they would bang into the bank, and Billy would cuss softly. Art convinced his partner that they would have to leave the light on all of the time. Things went a little better then.

It was only two miles to the spot where they planned to take the canoe out of the creek, but they hadn't figured on all of the switchbacks and turns the creek made. It was a warm night. There were clouds of mosquitoes in the swamp. Art alternately swatted and poled for what seemed like hours as the creek meandered back and forth through the cedars. Even Bill had never been up the creek this far before. His voice didn't have that bold confidence that Art was used to hearing when he answered Art's questions.

"How much farther is it?"

"How the hell do I know?"

"Are you sure we didn't take the wrong fork?"

"I sure hope not."

"Where are all the deer?"

"They're not out tonight."

"Where are they when they're in?"

"I'll ask my uncle."

"How much longer will those batteries last?"

"Not much longer."

Just about the time they were wishing they had never started out on this trip, the dim orange beam from the dying flashlight picked up the soft glow of two eyes. They were well back from the creek. It was a long shot. Billy raised his rifle and drew a bead right between the eyes. Carefully, he squeezed off a round. The .22 cracked. The eyes disappeared. Billy stepped out onto the stream bank and vanished off into the inky darkness to check his kill.

Art sat shivering in the back of the canoe. He was covered with mosquito bites, scared and excited. It seemed like an hour, but in a few minutes he felt the canoe rock as Billy got back in.

Art asked, "Did you kill it?"

Billy said, "Yup."

"Where did you hit it?" Art asked.

Billy said, "Right between the eyes."

"Is it a buck or a doe?" Art inquired.

Billy replied very softly, "It's my pony."

The canoe had drifted out of the cedars and right up behind the Ness barn without the boys realizing where they were. The pony was standing in the barn with its head out over the lower half of the two-piece dutch door when Bill shot. It was dead before its knees buckled. That was the night Art discovered that Billy Ness wasn't perfect after all.

Art Gillette went on to become a game warden. I ran into him when I was transferred to the southern part of the state where he was my supervisor. One evening, over a few beers, he told me the story of Billy and his pony.

***

My dad was the strongest personality I've ever known. He's been dead 25 years, but hardly a day goes by that I don't think of him. I grew up watching every move he made and feeling that he was watching every move I made.

He was a superb hunter and marksman. I saw him make several long-range shots on running game that were almost unbelievable. Some of the happiest moments of my youth were spent sitting in his deer camp, listening to him and his hunting partners discussing past hunts and planning new ones. I was proud of the fact that he was the acknowledged leader of the crew.

It seemed I was always trying to satisfy and please him, but never succeeding. I only recall him telling me how I could have done it better. That's why I was surprised and truly happy when I discovered that he was proud that his kid had become a game warden. I was also a little surprised because I knew that once in a while his hunting crew had some illegal meat hidden out under a brush pile. Game wardens were frequently discussed around his camp, and I don't remember much of it being very complimentary.

After I went to work and got stationed in the same county his deer camp was in, he told me that I should tell all my warden friends that there would be hot coffee for them anytime they wanted to stop in. I knew that this also meant that there would never be any illegal meat under the brush piles again.

One cold winter day, my folks drove up to Superior for dinner. This was a rare occasion, so my wife was preparing quite a feast. Just about the time we were going to sit down and eat, I got a phone call. It was the police department dispatcher reporting that a car had hit a deer on the east edge of town. I knew that if I didn't go pick it up, I'd get five more phone calls about it during dinner. I told my wife to hold the meal and that I'd be back in half an hour. My dad said he'd ride along.

When we got to the accident site, there were at least 50 cars pulled over alongside the road. A wrecker and a squad car had their red lights running; a cop was directing traffic. Countless people were lined up on the shoulder of the road. They were looking out onto a baseball diamond that had a foot of new snow on it. There stood a fawn with three broken legs. All three legs were snapped off a few inches above the hooves, and when the fawn would try to walk, the broken ends flopped and banged around, bringing a collective moan of sympathy from the crowd.

As I walked through the crowd I could hear people saying things like, "Oh good, the game warden is here." I know what they were thinking. They were just sure I'd walk out there and pick the poor little thing up and carry it away to the baby deer hospital where it would be made all better. I knew I was going to kill it and that I wasn't going to be popular with them.

I made a brief public explanation of how there was no possible way to help the fawn, and so I was going to put it out of its misery as quickly as possible. There were a lot of disappointed looks passed around as I returned to the car to get my rifle. My old man said, "These people aren't going to like you."

I discovered that my rifle wasn't in the car. The only firearm I had was a .38 caliber snub-nosed revolver in the glove compartment. The gun was accurate only at point blank range and had very little energy. This wasn't going to make things any easier.

Because of several nearby houses and the short range of the pistol, I had to get close to the deer for an accurate shot. I walked towards it very slowly. When I got within 25 yards, it turned and tried to run. A loud cry rose from the crowd. I stopped and the deer stopped. Each time I tried to move closer it would again try to run. The snow was speckled with blood along the trail we were making as I continued to try to get in range for a killing shot.

Out in deep right field it became apparent that I would not be able to sneak up on Bambi. A change in tactics was required. I calculated that I could probably run faster than the crippled deer could, so I'd have to rush it. I hoped I could catch it quickly and dispatch it with one fast shot. I calculated incorrectly. The damned thing could run just as fast as I could. It raced around the ball field with those stub legs flopping and blood spurting everywhere. I was just able to keep pace as we zigzagged along like the characters in a Keystone Cops episode.

Now, the crowd took on the characteristics of an old-time lynch mob. I wondered if my dad had joined them. They were getting mad, but so was I. I was also getting winded. I put on my last good burst of speed when the deer fell while trying to turn. I got to the fawn as it was struggling to get up. I pounced on it and flattened it. Then I put the muzzle of the snub-nose in its ear and pulled tile trigger. It cried out like a baby lamb separated from its mother. I pumped four more rounds through its head for good measure. Finally, it was dead.

I sat in the snow, panting for breath and looking at all those people booing, shaking their fists and screaming at me as if I had dropped an easy fly ball with the bases loaded. I thought, "So you wanted to be a game warden, eh?" I was glad the police were still there when I dragged the little carcass up to my car.

Yeah, I should have had a better gun in the car and I should have had the police disperse those people before I killed the deer. But dinner was waiting and I was in a hurry. What the hell, nobody is perfect.

On the way home my old man grinned and said, "This is quite a job that you've got." I couldn't help but think that, once again, I hadn't impressed him very favorably.

***

Clyde Custer wasn't perfect either, but he was pretty damned good. He rose quickly through the ranks of the warden force. Clyde brought more enthusiasm to the job, even on his last few days of work before retiring, than most rookies did on their first day. He's been retired for years but, he's still got a lot of game warden in him.

Clyde was a big, rugged-looking guy that most women probably found to be handsome. He was a true student of the fish and game laws and could quote lengthy sections of the statutes from memory. Some of our attorneys would stop in and see him before they signed their legal interpretations.

I doubt that there was anyone on the force who was a harder charger than Custer. Whenever he saw the need, he advanced at full speed. Of course, people who respond this quickly sometimes make mistakes. That's what makes them interesting. Some of Clyde's exploits are legendary. If he had been perfect, he wouldn't have been nearly as much fun as he was, nor would he have been as popular with the wardens.

102

One of Clyde's imperfections was an extremely inventive vocabulary. There are a lot of words out there that he couldn't remember the exact meaning of, nor how they were pronounced. Being the hard-charger that he was, he wasn't deterred by this. He drove onward, injecting some of the most colorful semantics imaginable into his language.

His abuses of the English language would not have been nearly as startling, nor as amusing, if he weren't an intelligent man. He regularly spoke from a vast knowledge base, with passion and enthusiasm, injecting words that sort of sounded like the ones he wanted to use. The results were entertaining but did little for his presentation, which was invariably accurate and appropriate in thought. We loved it.

At a warden supervisors meeting one day he was lecturing us about the requirements for a search without a warrant. He twice repeated that it was important to make surreptitious observations. Unfortunately, both times he invented and used "surpastitious." Everyone smiled the first time, and giggled the second time he committed the mistake. He paused and laughed himself, knowing he had blown it. Some wag spoke out, "Clyde, are you sure you aren't Polish?" (Polish jokes were popular at the time.) He replied, "Naw, my wife just checked my gynecology tree and I'm pure German."

One day, a citizen wandered in off from the street with a question about the law. This was an administrative office and normally the public didn't drop in over such matters. It was more common to direct inquiries of this type out to the field offices. This citizen appeared to be slightly afflicted with Down's Syndrome, commonly referred to as a mongoloid.

Clyde was the picture of compassion. He patiently explained the rule over and over again in the simplest terms possible, until it was finally clear to the fellow. Then he spent a few minutes visiting with him about his favorite fishing baits and even recommended a good hot spot where he knew the fish were biting. It was touching to watch Clyde accompany the man to the door with his arm around his shoulder and wish him the best of luck on his fishing trip. Custer returned to his office sadly shaking his head and said, "The poor devil is a Mongolian."

Around the office we began identifying these miscues as "custerisms," and I even took notes on them. Why not? They were precious, and you might only hear them once. My favorite all-time best custerism was overheard during a telephone conversation between Clyde and Colonel Goetsch, who was the chief of the State Patrol.

We had nice uniforms. They were made of good, hard-finish gabardine and cost the state an arm and a leg. Clyde was searching for a way to trim our growing costs, and the uniforms were a good place to start. He had called the company that manufactured them for us. They told him that the main reason that we were paying so much was that our uniform material was very distinctive and that they didn't use it for any other customers but us. They had to buy and store huge bolts of the material and keep it in stock until we sent in an order. They suggested that we either change to a lower cost, more popular fabric or that we buy the material and store it ourselves. We could simply send them the required amount of cloth with each uniform order. They finished by saying that our State Patrol had the same problem.

Clyde got Colonel Goetsch on the phone and was suggesting that the two organizations should get together and acquire a proper storage area for the material. The two agencies could share the storage and both would reap a considerable cost savings. (This is the kind of thinking that makes good administrators. The program was eventually adopted and the taxpayers saved a good deal of money.)

I was sitting in Custer's office and listening in on his conversation with Goetsch. I winced a little when he told the colonel that we would have to make sure that the storage area was "venom proof." Maybe the colonel hadn't noticed the slip, I hoped. Within a few minutes the boss repeated the need for "venom proof" storage. I couldn't keep my nose out of it any longer. "Psst, Clyde," I interrupted. He covered the mouthpiece of the phone with his hand and said, "Yeah, what do you want?" I asked him, "Don't you mean vermin proof?" He asked, "Vermin, ain't that mice?" I said that, yup, it was. He said, "No, I mean venom proof," and went back to his conversation. I never did figure out what he was getting at, but I learned to mind my own business.

Clyde was a Navy veteran. Maybe he was a frogman or something. He was the kind of guy who would volunteer to be shot out of the torpedo tube in his swimming suit and cut submarine nets with a Swiss Army knife.

During his early days on the warden force, Custer was a holy terror. He worked in the Fox River Valley where there were a lot of fish and a lot of fish pirates. If anybody ever figured out how to be in two places at once, it would be him. There are some marvelous stories told by older wardens who worked with him at the time. One of my favorites is told by Dave Frogatt, who served under Clyde during his probationary period.

It seems that some outlaw had placed a big fish trap in a creek right under a bridge in Clyde's area. A cooperative citizen had seen the trap and reported its location to Warden Custer. The way fish traps work, one must let them sit a while as fish move into them slowly. If they are well placed they will yield quite a haul after a few hours. Clyde knew that this greedy outlaw would likely return after dark to reap his harvest. Warden Custer intended to be there waiting when the guy returned.

The tactical problem with this particular violation was that the bridge where the trap was set was on a quiet road and nearly everyone living along the road was a fish pirate. If a warden even drove his car down the road, the telephone would ring in every house announcing the presence of the lawman. If they were seen by anyone, the trap would not be tended that night. Clyde devised a scheme for getting into the area undetected.

He collected a thermos jug of coffee, a flashlight, his binoculars and his ticket book. He called Dave Frogatt and instructed him to be at Clyde's house a half-hour before sunset.

Later, he explained to Dave how Mrs. Custer would drive a borrowed station wagon over the bridge just after dark. Surely nobody would recognize the car. She would not stop but would simply slow down while the wardens would jump out and run hide in the bushes along the creek. Here they would wait for the fish trapper to arrive.

A few minutes later, Mrs. Custer drove the borrowed wagon down the quiet road at 50 miles per hour with two game wardens sitting on the tailgate. When she neared the bridge, Clyde told her to slow down to exactly 30 miles per hour. Dutifully, she held the speedometer needle right on 30 as she rumbled over the bridge. Clyde gathered up an armload of equipment and hollered, "Go," and boosted himself off from the tailgate.

Now exiting backwards at 30 miles per hour is quite a trick, even for a Navy frogman. Dave sat on the tailgate watching as his boss rolled end over end down the gravel road, making a tremendous dust cloud. In the eerie red glow of the taillights he saw the thermos bottle, ticket book, and the binoculars appear alternately, but briefly, out of the cloud. He asked Mrs. Custer to please stop the car and he walked back towards the dust as the wagon drove on.

He found Custer standing unsteadily in the middle of the road. He was bleeding from several scrapes and bruises on his face and hands, and his jacket was ripped up the seam in the back. He was covered with dirt and dust and a piece of gravel was imbedded in his forehead. He held his elbow in a sort of funny way.

Dave picked up the thermos and gave it a shake. It emitted a tinkling sound. So did the binoculars. "Are you OK?' he asked Clyde. "Of course," Custer replied. "I learned to roll like that in the Navy."

Dave never did say whether the fish trapper showed up or not.

For a while, Custer was involved in the education and training of the department's law officers. He organized and standardized the training of recruit wardens and maintained a recurrent training program for all of the wardens. The work was long overdue and he did an excellent job of bringing some order to this important part of our occupation.

One day, he told a large recruit class that he would demonstrate the proper technique for unloading a canoe from the roof of a moving automobile and launching it on a dead run. The other instructors were startled as they were unaware that we had such a technique. The recruits eyed each other warily in anticipation of the attempt.

Clyde explained how the purpose of the exercise was to quickly get the canoe in the water without being noticed by any "unfriend-lies" who may live in the area. He said that a two-man crew and a driver were required. From the class he selected two likely look-ing recruits for partners, and they held a briefing while the rest of the class adjourned to the field for the demonstration.

Clyde's plan was that they would drive the auto at exactly 20 miles per hour. The canoe would be strapped to a carrier on the roof. Clyde would ride in the right front seat of the car, his helper directly behind him. At Clyde's signal, both men would reach out their respective windows and unfasten the straps that secured the craft. As they approached the creek, Clyde would step out the door and start sprinting. He would slide the canoe off from the roof and hold it over his head and, followed by his helper, would veer off towards the creek and dive through the air, twisting deftly so that the canoe would hit the water right side up with both men in it.

With the remainder of the class lined up along the road, the demonstration began. It is said that wagering against the success of the mission was heavy among the recruits.

Under the circumstances, 20 miles per hour looked awfully fast as the sedan with a canoe upside down on the roof approached the bridge over the creek. Suddenly the right front door flew open and there was instructor Clyde at top speed. Then, almost unbeliev-ably, the canoe was over his head at arm's length as he sprinted alongside the car. This guy was fast and athletic. It began to look as though this remarkable feat might be accomplished. No one was more surprised at the successful beginning of the trick than the recruit in the back seat. Remembering his role in the plan, he threw open the back door in preparation of his exit.

Clyde hooked the back of his heel on the door that had suddenly been opened behind him and fell on his face. There was a sickening crunch as both Clyde and a 13-foot aluminum canoe jammed past under the open door. The man and the wreckage slid to a stop in the middle of the bridge and the bets were paid off.

Theodore Roosevelt said: "Far better it is to dare mighty deeds, to win glorious triumphs, even though checkered with failures, than to take rank with those unfortunate souls who neither enjoy much nor suffer much, for they live in the gray twilight that knows not victory nor defeat."

Clyde never spent five minutes in that gray twilight.

Chapter 9

AIR SUPPORT

There was a lot of excitement in our outfit when the first air-planes were purchased in 1957. Some of the wardens figured the new machines would solve all of their problems. They wouldn't have to patrol at all anymore. They could just sit by the radio and wait for a call from the pilot and then casually drive out and write the tickets.

On the other end of things were a few wardens who had decided that the contraptions were useless. The state paid almost $8000 for each of them. To those guys, the planes represented the reason that there was no money left in the budget to replace the rickety outboard motor or the leaky boat that they had been issued. As it turned out, neither opinion was very well founded but there was a little dab of truth in each.

The Champion Aircraft Company manufactured our first planes. The company called this model the "Challenger," but everybody in the outfit called them "Champs." They were fabric-covered, high-winged two-seaters. They were powered by a 150 horse-power Lycoming engine that sounded, to the occupants, like 600 horses. As airplanes go, these were noisy and they were slow. The slow part was usually an advantage, but sometimes an aggrava-tion.

Each one was equipped with three radios: one for talking to control towers and flight service stations, one for navigation and one for talking to game wardens. There was also a public address system with an external loud speaker for hollering at folks on the ground. The planes had skis with a hydraulic pump that could raise or lower them a few inches for landing on snow-covered surfaces or bare ground. One of the planes had floats for water landings. Another had a big, heavy aerial mapping camera mounted in the back end.

By the time the pilot tossed in his thermos bottle and binoculars and put on the parachute that was required for all night flights, the little ship was overloaded. According to the manual, it wouldn't fly. It didn't matter, though. The little Champ just shuddered down the runway a couple hundred feet further and then lugged all that junk up in the air and went to work.

The planes were used primarily for patrol work and spent lots of hours down below 500 feet of altitude. That is also the favorite altitude for about 95 percent of the flying insects in the world. The windshield and leading edges of the wings were always coated with a quarter-inch compaction of bug carcasses. This prompted one pilot to refer to his Champ as "The Bug Smasher." Another pilot told him that he was lucky that the plane was so slow. It probably only killed the bugs that were flying in the opposite direction that he was. Otherwise there would be twice as many of them smacked on there.

One day I opened the cowling of my Champ to check the oil and found a neatly lettered message painted on the fire wall. "This aircraft is not faster than a speeding bullet, nor a cow." I bet one of those wiseacre mechanics did it.

The Champs were tough little birds and we asked an awful lot of them. They flew in all kinds of weather and did all kinds of jobs. And they never failed to bring us home safely when it was over. A couple of them got bent up pretty badly, but it was never their fault. It was usually because some pilot tried to do something that he, and perhaps no other pilot in the world, could quite pull off.

The department decreed that all of the pilots must first be game wardens. Earle Gingles, before he became a game warden, was a P-38 pilot in World War II. Earle was a soft-spoken, studious sort of fellow. It took a lot to get him excited. Tall, slim and sandy-haired, he was a natural choice as one of the first to be promoted to warden/pilot. He could fly a Champ better than anyone I ever rode with, and I rode with dozens of them.

He was fussy about the plane's maintenance and was a careful and safe pilot. It didn't look as if he was being careful when he'd slip that thing in over the trees and set it down in your driveway, but he was. He was just really good and knew exactly how good he was.

In January, the bays and harbors along the south shore of Lake Superior freeze over. Hundreds of fishermen venture out there and try to bob a few lake trout through a hole in the ice. This is one of the coldest parts of the country, and only the hardiest of fishermen can be found there, unless the weather is unseasonably mild.

The warden in Bayfield had contacted three of his neighboring wardens; they had plans to check all of the ice fishermen they could find one Sunday. The weather was forecasted to be sunny and calm. They asked Earle to fly along the south shore to locate the concentrations of fishermen. This would save them a lot of driving time and assure that they could get a look at most of the anglers out there on this rare, pleasant winter day.

The trouble was, nature didn't cooperate. Although it wasn't bitter cold, there was a low, gray overcast and a blustery west wind. Gingles pointed the Champ west out of Saxon Harbor and dropped down to 500 feet. He called on the radio and established contact with the group of wardens.

Looking down, Earle had difficulty making out the ice surface. It was snow- covered and about the same color as the sky. When he looked out over the big lake there was no visible horizon. Clouds of blowing snow whipped along below him and further obscured his vision. He could only see the dark objects such as the rocky shoreline and the occasional chunk of driftwood that stuck up through the ice. When the wind let up periodically, he could see long ice ridges and snowdrifts running parallel to his direction of flight. When it blew very hard he lost sight of everything temporarily and had to use his instruments to maintain the plane's attitude.

111

Whenever he flew through the scud of clouds, rime ice formed quickly on the frontal surfaces of the plane. The carburetor also iced up unless he kept the heat knob out halfway.

Soon he spotted two fishermen a few hundred yards off shore. He called one of the wardens and a car was immediately dispatched to the location. The Champ continued on to the west. As other small groups of fishermen were located, Gingles relayed their positions to a warden, and in spite of poor weather and a lack of large concentrations, the work continued.

He flew over a pair of fishermen a few miles west of Bayfield. They had snowmobiles parked near the holes they had cut, and he saw several fish laying on the ice around them. In an instant the men were lost from view in the blowing snow. Not exactly sure of his position, Gingles began a circle that would take him back over the men a second time. He hated to do that because most outlaws would tolerate only one pass from the plane. If it circled for a second look, they were sure it was one of the department's new flying game wardens and they would quickly clean up their act.

On the second pass he had dropped down to 200 feet and caught a quick but clearer look at them. There were dozens of fish on the ice, and they looked like trout. These guys had found a great spot. The fish were biting like crazy. Earle guessed that there were two or three times as many trout on the ice as the law allowed.

His radio call brought bad news. All of the wardens were miles away checking the other fishermen. It would be over an hour before anyone could get there. He pulled the Champ up to 2000 feet and began a holding pattern several miles east of the snowmobiles. There was nothing to do but wait until one of the wardens showed up and hope that the two fish pirates were still down there. He also hoped that the weather wouldn't worsen because it was already marginal.

Earle poured himself a cup of coffee and looked down. There was a layer of thin, broken clouds between him and the ground. He was sure the men could not see the plane. He had set his holding pattern downwind from them so they would not hear the Champ's engine. He continued to circle.

Several minutes later he was looking down through a hole in the clouds and he saw two snowmobiles racing along the shore towards Bayfield. The snowmobile was a brand new gadget in those days and there were very few of them around. The odds were good that these were his pirates. He pointed the nose of the Champ down and headed for the spot where they had been fishing. A couple circles around the area confirmed his belief. They were gone.

Earle started east along the frozen beach. Again he called on the radio for some help. It was still no use. The wardens were almost half an hour away. By then the snow machines would be back in town.

Within minutes, Gingles overtook the speeding sleds. He was going with the wind now, and they were in sight for only an instant as he flashed past.

If Earle had been only a pilot, not a game warden, he would have given up right here. He'd have considered that the weather was terrible and the situation was such that the bad guys were going to get away this time. But he was a game warden and he never hesitated.

After he passed the snowmobiles, Gingles continued along the shoreline for 90 seconds. Then he banked the Champ on a wing tip, turned it 180 degrees, leveled the wings and pulled the throttle back to about half power. He was about 150 feet above the ice and settling gradually towards the surface, but he usually couldn't see it. He was heading into the wind now and when he could see the ice he could tell that his ground speed was very slow.

He put the flaps down a couple notches and pumped the skis into landing position. Between wind gusts he saw some long ice ridges, now about 50 feet below him. He moved the Champ over a few feet so that he would land between them. A blast of wind kicked up a big cloud of loose snow and Gingles was on instruments again. He closed the throttle completely and leveled the wings on the plane's artificial horizon. The Champ settled softly on the snow-covered ice about a quarter of a mile ahead of the oncoming snowmobiles.

There was an expensive-sounding crunch as the right landing gear slammed into an unseen ice ridge. The plane spun around in a circle to the right and started to tip up on its nose. Gingles was thrown forward into his shoulder harness. The plane teetered for a moment and then dropped back down on the skis. Earle still couldn't see through the snow any further than the wing tips. All he knew for sure was that he was unhurt and that this landing could probably be classified as a crash.

He got out and looked around. The right landing gear was bent out and to the rear far enough that the plane sat badly tilted to the right. The right wing tip was only about a foot above the snow. The ski was still attached to the axle but somehow it had inverted and was "snow side" up. There was a dent in the leading edge of the right wing and a hole about a foot square in the center of the windshield.

Shortly after the snow settled, the snowmobiles pulled up alongside the badly bent flying machine. Gingles asked, "How many trout have you guys got?" They had way too many. They were so dazzled by the warden's dramatic arrival that they didn't argue about anything. After he had issued each of them a citation, they offered him a ride to town.

Instead, Gingles completed a thorough inspection of the plane and concluded that, with some work, it might be flyable. His new friends got under the right wing and picked it up high enough for him to swing the ski around the axle to its normal position. This reduced the Champ's starboard list by about half. He borrowed the cover of a plastic bucket from one of the fishermen and taped it over the hole in the windshield. After he'd done some wiring and bracing, he checked the dent in the wing. It didn't look too serious.

The fishermen cut a bunch of pine branches and stuck them in the snow in two long, parallel lines, outlining a smooth section of lake surface for a runway. They waved good bye as the sagging plane wallowed away, lifted off and disappeared into the blowing snow. Two hours later the Champ was in its hangar. Gingles was starting on his second beer and working on the story he was going to have to tell to the chief warden and the Federal Aviation Agency. They were both pretty tough customers to deal with.

***

A little west of Oshkosh, several thousand Canada geese had moved in and made themselves at home on Elizabeth Lake. Elizabeth was a good waterfowl hunting lake and over the years countless limits of ducks and geese had been killed there. Millions of lead pellets from spent shotgun shells laid on the bottom in the shallow bays. The geese flew off in the daytime and fed on nearby grain fields. Later, they returned for water and to pick up grit for their gizzards. A good percentage of the grit that they picked up turned out to be lead BBs. The birds began to die of lead poisoning.

The department sent a crew of biologists over to camp on the lake and chase the geese off whenever they returned. The men would tear around the lake in a motor boat, hazing the geese into the air. The honkers would make one circle and settle back down behind the boat. After a few trips, the geese wouldn't even flush. They'd just hurry aside and let the boat go by. They liked it there and intended to stick around.

Ken Corbett was our pilot in Oshkosh. He heard about this problem and told the biologists that he would make a few low passes over the lake with his Champ, and it was likely that the geese would pull out. They were delighted and told him to go for it.

Corbett had the Champ clattering by daylight the next morning. As he neared the lake, he pushed the power to the red line and dropped down to about a hundred feet. The flock was gathered in a raft that covered almost 40 acres of the lake. He pointed at the center of the flock and let down a few more feet. He thundered over their heads and pulled up in a chandelle. Looking over his shoulder he saw a mild disturbance among the flock. Some of the geese were scurrying around on the water. The mob dispersed a bit and now covered about twice as big an area, but they weren't leaving.

On the next pass, Ken put the Champ right down among them. With the wheels barely out of the water, he again flew over the raft of geese. He watched ahead carefully now because if they should suddenly flush, he would have to pull up quickly to avoid hitting them. He'd read about airliners that had crashed after hitting a single goose. He could imagine what a 16-pound honker would do to his little fabric-covered craft. The birds hustled out of the way and let the Champ roar on past.

Corbett wasn't the sort of guy who accepted defeat gracefully. There had to be a way to do this. The public address system installed in the Champ was designed for police cars. It had an electronic siren feature. This time Ken turned on this siren and grabbed the microphone. He circled the lake and lined up for his next pass. A crowd of onlookers gathered along the shore couldn't believe their ears as the little plane roared across the water. The siren wailed, and Corbett's voice could be heard for two miles. "Get the hell out of here, you bastards!"

That did it. This time when he looked back the entire flock was in the air. He circled the lake and watched the milling birds. They circled the lake and watched the Champ. At an altitude of about 200 feet, the flyers eyed each other warily.

Suddenly the flock set their wings and started to settle back towards the lake. Ken turned towards the lake and started down also. The Champ got there first, but not by much. Corbett leveled out a foot or so above the water and turned on the siren. He found the sky above him was nearly solid feathers. It seemed as if the entire sky was covered with milling geese only a few feet above his wings.

Now he was worried. The birds were acting crazy. Some dove down and splashed on the lake surface in front of him. Others pulled up steeply as he approached them. Most of them found it necessary to empty their bowels with the strain of their maneuvers. The first load of goose poop centered the windshield with a loud splat. Other gobs hit the wings and the tail surfaces. Then he was flying through curtains of the stuff. By now, Corbett wanted out of this deal. He was tearing along about 90 miles per hour between two deadly layers, one of water and one of geese. Hitting either one would mean a fatal crash, and there was very little room between them. He had no choice but to continue straight ahead.

Several times he was sure of the crash, but at the last instant either he or a goose was able to dip a wing and avoid the collision by inches. It seemed like hours but it was more like 20 seconds when, breaking into a sweat, he flew out from under the flock. He climbed up a bit and continued straight ahead until he regained his composure. When he turned back he saw the geese had scattered in all directions. They weren't circling either. They were looking for a new home.

As he was flying back towards the office, Ken thought about how businesslike those biologists always were. Every time they did anything, they sat down afterwards and wrote a paper on it. He had plenty of time to prepare his report to them. After what he'd been through, he was going to get some mileage out of this.

He sat at his desk sucking on his pipe as an excited biologist, who had been at the lake, told everyone in the office how thrilling the air show was. He raved on about Corbett's skill and daring as he flung his frail little craft at the geese. He said that Ken's determined efforts had chased the birds from the lake for good and surely saved thousands of them from a slow death from lead poisoning.

When the biologist finally finished, Corbett explained how he instinctively knew that the only way to evict the birds was to get the plane between them and the water and make all of the noise he possibly could. He said that the operation was really quite routine and that he found it necessary to fly in that manner nearly every day. "If you'll excuse me now, I must write a new section for the flight manual on how to haze geese," he said. And to himself he said, "I wouldn't do that again for all the tea in China."

***

We used the Champs to find lost hunters, patrol closed areas, do surveys, check forest fires and countless other chores. The longer we had them, the more tricks we learned to do with them. The plane was the most useful, however, when it came to finding deer shiners.

A warden in a car on the ground could normally spot a deer shiner two or three miles away. He could hear the outlaw shoot at about the same range. A pilot in an airplane up at about 6000 feet could normally spot a shiner 15 or more miles away. Occasionally, under the right conditions, they could be seen at twice that distance. Not just any pilot could do it. But a game warden who had worked on deer shiners for years, and was now a warden/pilot, could.

The normal procedure was to station four wardens' cars in an area where there had been illegal night hunting. The cars were usually set in a box pattern. Each side of the square was about 10 or 15 miles long. The pilot would then circle just outside of the box. He could effectively cover visually about 15 miles on each side of the plane. It took about 40 minutes to make the circuit, and he was patrolling over 1500 square miles.

When he found somebody who was working a light, there was always a warden within 15 miles of the suspect. Using the radio, he would then direct the field warden to the light and the bad guys were had. During the first couple of years that we had the Champs, we caught hundreds of deer shining outlaws across the northern half of the state.

I'd been fascinated with airplanes since I was a little kid. I suppose I made and flew a thousand model planes. My father was a pilot and owned a small two-place Cessna. Within a few days of my 16th birthday I soloed his plane. As the years passed, a lot of things kept me from seriously pursuing aviation. I never got away from it completely, however, and when I became a warden I started logging more flight time. I had my eye on one of those flying warden jobs.

In 1969 they gave me wings. I was promoted to warden/pilot and transferred to the state's southern district.

For decades, the major portion of the deer herd had been in the central and northern counties of the state. At about the time I moved south, the deer population there was beginning to increase dramatically.

Most of the local bandits hadn't yet discovered the thrill and rewards of shining deer. That was just as well because most of the wardens down there didn't know how to catch deer shiners yet, either.

Things changed quickly. It wasn't long before the guys were getting calls about gun shots in the night and finding gut piles in the alfalfa fields the next morning. Suddenly, the warden force in the southern district was working nights.

One of the first shining outfits that we caught with the airplane was in Sauk County. Warden Harley asked me to fly a pattern over three cars in the northeast corner of his county.

We got started about an hour before midnight. The Champ carried enough fuel to work the area for over four hours and still get back to the airport with a safe margin of gas remaining. It was a clear, calm night and I could see the lights of towns 50 miles away. I trimmed the plane for level flight at 6500 feet and started circling to locate the wardens. One by one, they flashed a light up at me as I passed over them. When I had their positions fixed I started around the pattern.

It was a Saturday night. There was a lot of traffic. When there was a bunch of cars moving down there it was always difficult to pick out the hunters' flashlights. I wound my way around the area for over three hours and didn't see a thing worth checking out. I poured some coffee and turned around to work the pattern in the opposite direction. It didn't really matter which way I went, but the small change in the routine helped keep me awake.

Early in the flight, the wardens were all business on the radio. There was only one airplane in the district and 25 wardens vied for the use of it. They knew that this was their best chance to catch a shining outfit, as they may not get the plane over them again for another month.

They didn't really want people to shine deer, but if people were going to do it, they wanted to catch them at it. From the complaints they were receiving from rural home owners, they knew there was some night hunting going on. As the night wore on, they began to sound less optimistic about their chances.

Now the tavern lights began to go out. It was past closing time and I could see more headlights as the revelers made their way home from the bars. This was the time when the real outlaws went deer hunting.

The traffic thinned to a trickle. The countryside grew darker. Soon the only lights visible were the blue mercury vapor lights on the end of barns. Another hour slipped by and northeast Sauk County was still peaceful. I called the guys and told them I was getting low on fuel and we should call it off. I watched their headlights come on as they scattered for home.

Turning the Champ towards the Madison airport, I started a slow descent. I could see the flash of the airport beacon in the clear night air. Later, I glanced down and saw a small, dim streak of light shine out the side of a slow-moving vehicle directly below me.

I called warden Harley and told him to turn around and come back. I suggested that he should come down Highway 23. There was a customer down there he'd probably like to talk to.

As I climbed back to cruising altitude, the car below me turned west and began shining again. Through my binoculars, I could see that he was on a farm road and was shining the light into a green field. The car continued along slowly. Every few minutes the occupants would look over another field.

The brake lights lit up when the car stopped again, and the light shone steadily across a field. Then the car drove off the road and out into the field, stopped, and the lights were switched off.

If they had seen or shot a deer, I wouldn't be able to tell from 6500 feet. We flew at this altitude for several reasons. It was the best altitude to see lights at a good distance. It also put us up where the plane attracted little attention. In case of an engine failure at night, the extra altitude also gave us some additional time to consider our options. (Jump and pull the ripcord? Chancy at night. A dead-stick landing in a field you could barely see? Even chancier.) Sometimes you wished that you were down a lot lower so that you could see better and figure out what was going on. This was one of those times.

I called Harley again and checked on his progress. He was still miles to the north. He had been almost home when I turned him around. I gave him an up-to-the-minute report on the outfit I'd been watching.

Then I looked at my gas gauge. It said zero. I rocked the wings and the needle bobbed up off the zero and then settled back on the peg again. I'd landed with the gauge in this condition before and found, when I filled the tank, that there was still three or four gallons left. The most accurate estimate of remaining fuel is determined by time in the air. The gauge is used mostly to confirm your computation. The way I figured it, I had a little over 30 minutes of fuel remaining, and the airport was 15 minutes away. I leaned the fuel mixture a little more.

I continued to circle the dark spot where I had seen the car's headlights go off several minutes ago. I told Harley to hurry or else he was going to find the Champ and the shiners in the same alfalfa field.

The car lights came back on below me as the deer shiner drove east to Highway 23. He turned north. Although I hated to fly away from the airport any farther, I followed. It was after four a.m. now. There wasn't another vehicle anywhere in sight. I began to worry that the guy might pull into his yard and go to bed before Harley got there. I really didn't need another worry right then, either.

The guy was driving along at a normal rate of speed now. If he had been hunting, he was finished for the night. Finally, a set of south-bound headlights were visible up ahead. They were going like hell. I radioed Harley to flash his high beams down and up. It was him. Thanks a bunch, God.

I cranked the Champ around toward the beckoning airport beacon and watched back over my shoulder as the lights of the two vehicles continued towards each other. They were still a few miles apart when I told Harley that the next car he would meet would be the one that was shining. He said he'd stop them and look them over. I switched the radio off and figured out my remaining fuel. If everything was correct, I wouldn't make it.

I squirmed and sweated and held my breath. I called myself a stupid fool every minute or so. I knew how long this crate was supposed to stay up on a full tank. What was I doing up here when I was supposed to be down there? I stared at the airport beacon — it didn't seem to be getting any closer at all. Again I looked at the gas gauge and rocked the wings. The zero just sat there. There wasn't one more bounce in it. I rechecked the flight time for the 10th time and then watched Mickey's big hand go past the mark when I figured the Lycoming engine should quit. It was unfair how fast my watch seemed to run and how slow the airplane was going.

I looked down at Interstate 94 and told myself that when it quit, I'd try a dead stick landing on the nearly empty highway. I looked hard to see the concrete bridges that I knew crossed the pavement every few miles. I couldn't see them. Too dark. I'll bet that if a guy hit one of those . . . Ugh!

When the threshold lights of Runway 13 slipped under the Champ, I grinned from ear to ear. It was a terrible landing. I bounced five feet. The next morning I put 38.6 gallons of 80 octane aviation fuel in the Champ's 39-gallon tank.

Harley flipped on the siren and his flashing red light. The car immediately pulled over onto the shoulder of the road and stopped. The two young occupants were calm and almost friendly as the warden searched their car. He found a .300 Savage rifle in a case on the back seat. These guys were 15 miles north of the last field that they had shined. This warden had come from the north. He surely couldn't know what they had been up to. There was no law against having a rifle in the car, so they weren't worried. They asked him why he had stopped them. He said, "I just wanted to give you this ticket for shining deer with a gun in your possession."

The two men suggested to Harley that he must have mistakenly stopped the wrong car. They told a hastily contrived story which, they felt, confirmed their innocence. They said that they had been visiting friends in Madison that evening and were simply returning straight home. They denied that they had shined any deer. Their best efforts to talk Harley out of writing the ticket failed.

They plead "not guilty" in court the following day. A date was set for the trial and they hired an attorney. They told the lawyer that they had never shined deer and wondered how the warden thought he was going to prove that they had.

I flew back over the area in daylight the following day. The vehicle's drive tracks were plainly visible in the alfalfa field. I took some photos of the field to be used as evidence.

Harley was down there, following my directions, and he stopped his car right in the spot where the defendants had stopped the night before. There he found two empty .300 cartridge cases. When he followed the car tracks out into the field he discovered a fresh deer carcass. It had been gutted out, and some alfalfa plants had been uprooted and tossed over it. Apparently, they planned to return and pick it up later.

Additional charges, concerning the deer, were filed against the defendants. In his opening remarks, their attorney berated the local game warden and ranted on about the innocence of his clients. He briefly outlined their story about driving straight home from Madison.

When the district attorney said that his first witness would be the pilot of the airplane who had followed the defendants around while they were shining, the defense immediately asked for a recess.

"Airplane?" one of them mumbled. There was a lot of whispering and head shaking. They didn't know there was an airplane involved. "I wonder what they can see from up there," their attorney muttered. In a few minutes the huddle broke up. Their attorney told the court that his clients would like to change their plea to "guilty" on all charges.

After court, the lawyer told Harley that he could have saved a lot of time if he had told everyone about the "air support" a lot earlier. Harley said, "I figured I would tell you at the disclosure hearing, but you didn't request a hearing."

When we left, the lawyer was mad at the outlaws for lying to him and embarrassing him in court. The convicted men were mad at him because he hadn't asked for a disclosure hearing, although they had no idea what a disclosure hearing was. I was still mad at myself for nearly running the Champ out of gas. Harley was smiling. He wasn't mad at anybody. He had his shining outfit in the bag.

***

Eventually we wound up with quite an air force: 26 airplanes and 16 pilots. We had a large maintenance facility in Madison with four full-time mechanics. We had a DC-3 and seven other twin-engine airplanes plus a bunch of military surplus stuff and the Champs. I got a promotion and was spending most of my time flying dignitaries around the country.

It began to strike people as strange that the state owned 26 airplanes and 26 of them belonged to the Department of Natural Resources. The bureaucrats knew how to solve that. They took them all away from us. If a game warden needs an airplane to work deer shiners today, the DNR has to rent a Champ (which we had already bought and paid for) from the state Department of Administration.

Once again, things just weren't quite as much fun as they used to be. It was about this time that I quit flying and went to work in the DNR Law Enforcement Bureau's undercover section.

Chapter 10

UNDERCOVER

As far back as the late 1920s, and perhaps earlier, game wardens occasionally got out of uniform and into civilian clothes to do a little undercover enforcement work. They had discovered that this was a great way to gather evidence against the more serious violators. They couldn't do it in their own backyard, of course; they were very well known locally. Usually the local warden talked another warden from a few counties away into helping him with problems like this.

More often than not, they simply patronized a tavern that was a hangout for the suspects. If everything went well, they became trusted friends of the outlaws and soon had enough rope with which to hang them.

In the early 1930s, two Wisconsin wardens were appointed to full-time covert investigative work. They did not have specific areas assigned but worked statewide. Society in general knew very little of undercover enforcement. The unwary crooks were not looking for undercover game wardens, and it was easy for them to befriend suspects. The entrapment defense was not in common use as it is today. Times were hard and a lot of illegal trade in deer and ducks was going on. All of these factors combined to make these early investigators remarkably successful.

After a few productive years and the prosecution of several commercial violators, the word got around that the wardens had a "dirty tricks squad." Then the job got a little tougher. New faces were added to the undercover group and, by carefully selecting his case assignments, it was possible to keep a warden in this program for as long as five years. By that time he had been seen in too many bars and courtrooms to conceal his identity any longer. He was also probably getting sick of the clandestine nature of his job by that time.

I joined this group in 1979 and spent five years as an investigator and another five as the chief of what had come to be known as the Special Investigations Section. This was a really interesting period of time to be involved in covert enforcement. Commercial wildlife crime had become a serious problem. The black-market prices on everything from eagle feathers to bear gall bladders had gone right through the roof.

The illegal trade became a high priority issue with us, and we were given additional manpower, equipment and budgets. Throughout the entire law enforcement community, the decade of the '80s saw tremendous strides in undercover technology and techniques. Special long-range photography equipment, listening devices, tiny transmitters that could easily be hidden on a person, videotape equipment, night-vision scopes, computers and specialized surveillance vehicles equipped with all of the above toys were in common use by the better enforcement agencies. That included us.

At this time, we sort of graduated from single individual efforts against these criminal activities to larger, organized investigations. I mean the type of thing that the newspapers like to call "sting operations." What we were doing was devising methods that allowed us to look at large groups of suspects and quickly sort out the bad apples.

The efforts of this small group of lawmen had a large-scale, positive, long-lasting effect on the wildlife resources of the state. It was also a hell of a lot of fun sometimes.

Undercover game wardens are a separate breed altogether. Of course, they never wear uniforms. Their badge lies in a drawer at home most of the time. They don't get their pictures in the newspaper anymore, and while they may now make the biggest and best busts of their careers, they are never publicly recognized for their accomplishments.

They acquire a new identity — a new name, address, occupation and background. It's all a lie, of course. They carefully guard against revealing their true identity when they are working. Not only do they tell a lot of lies while they're working, but they also must conceal their occupation from new acquaintances and neighbors. Even their wives and children get good at giving vague answers about why the old man is gone so much of the time.

All of this is stressful to these guys, and the crowning touch comes when they discover that they are now divorced from the regular game warden fraternity. By now you probably understand that most wardens are ego-driven. They feed on public recognition of their work as much as anything. The moral support of their peers and the friendly competition among them is a comforting factor. When they go undercover, they become isolated from their support group as well as from the public.

Now they seek out and keep company with the antisocial element of this business. They spend most of their working hours with a bunch of shaggy creeps whom they dislike intensely. They may spend days with them, sleeping in the same shack and eating at the same table. They will try to remember every word that is said and guard every word that they say themselves. They will do their best to appear as though they are doing neither.

When things go poorly, they have no one to nurture them, and when things go well, nobody to share it with. It takes a pretty stable and confident person or a total flake to be good at this.

***

Generally speaking, it is unlawful to buy or sell wildlife. The practice is also very offensive socially. When we prosecuted commercial violators, the department usually received strong public support. Convictions for the crime carry the highest penalties in fish and game law.

There are a few exceptions to this general prohibition on wild-life commerce. One of the most notable is commercial fishing. Lakes Superior and Michigan are the two largest bodies of fresh water in the world. Whitefish, chubs, herring, perch and other species are netted lawfully by licensed commercial fishermen. The good ones work hard and make a lot of money. Why not? They are businessmen who don't have to pay a cent for their inventory. Nature, with a little help from the Department of Natural Resources, provides it for them.

There is also a small, fragile population of lake trout in these waters. They don't reproduce naturally and so the population is generated in several fish hatcheries. A very limited catch of these fish is allowed in Lake Superior, but they are protected from netting altogether in Lake Michigan.

For as long as there have been both wardens and nets, there has been a running battle with the commercial fisherman over the lake trout. Some greedy outlaw is always dropping a gill net in good trout water and sneaking a bunch of lakers to market. As is usually the case with protected species, they bring a higher price than most other fish in the lake. Field wardens do their best to police the activity, but those are awfully big lakes and there are a bunch of boats on them. The real careful crooks usually run their nets after dark. All of the advantages are with the illegal netter.

In the late 1970s, it was apparent from the activity in the fish shops that the lake trout black market was getting out of hand. The Special Investigations Section took a look at the problem.

Two investigators put an old icebox in the back of a pickup truck and passed themselves off as door-to-door salesmen. They began visiting commercial fishermen along the Great Lakes shore and making wholesale purchases of whitefish, supposedly for resale. They would then run across the state line to Chicago and sell the fish to the large markets there, recover the money they had spent and return to try another fisherman.

The undercover wardens always asked for legal species of fish and, the first time around, that's all that they got. After a couple of visits, some of the fishermen started offering them lake trout. The wardens were now in business. The illegal trout were frozen and stored as evidence. With fewer legal fish to re-sell to the Chicago markets, they quickly ran out of money.

Realizing that they had only scratched the surface, the wardens developed a plan. The department administrators listened to the idea and were a little skeptical. Several promises were made, which the investigators were not at all sure they could keep. Finally the administrators approved the scheme and forked over a pile of money. "Operation Gill Net" became our first project investigation.

We bought another truck and two large refrigerator units and painted our name on the sides. "Tri State Foods" became a pretty good customer for several crooked fishermen. We made a lot of mistakes at first, but the fish business was so dirty and we were so lucky that we got away with most of them.

Tri State Foods also rented a warehouse in Elgin, Illinois, and we put our name and logo on the building too. There, we received shipments of fish from commercial fishermen who were in the habit of delivering. To most folks, we looked like a legitimate business.

Soon we were regular providers of whitefish to the Chicago markets. The buyers in the markets began asking us for illegal lake trout, which they were getting from the other dealers. By this time we had enlisted the aid of the undercover staff from the Illinois Department of Conservation. They were very interested in prosecuting the Chicago markets, so we started selling some of the trout to the markets. Soon the Michigan Department of Natural Resources and the U.S. Fish and Wildlife Service became involved. Everyone brought a little more money and some more equipment to the project.

Nearly every new connection that we made provided another lead. It seemed as if the bigger we got, the bigger we got. We bought and sold fish, kept records, stored evidence and kept on truckin' for 22 months.

There are countless problems that materialize during one of these things. Lacking any previous experience, we sure had our share. We did realize early on that keeping all of this evidence sorted and in presentable shape was a very important issue. We had a bulging file of investigative reports, a spiral notebook full of scratchings that I never did understand, and hundreds of photographs. Finally we bought a video camera/recorder and started taping transactions whenever it was possible.

The first time we used the video was in the warehouse in Elgin. We were expecting a large shipment of illegal trout from a Lake Superior fisherman. Back in the corner of the warehouse there was a small toilet boarded off from the rest of the room. We cut a small hole in the sheetrock wall and set the camcorder up inside. From here we had a good view of the main entrance and the desk where the money would change hands. Shortly before the suspects were due, I went in the toilet and began waiting.

The bad guys arrived. There were two of them. One was obviously the brains of the outfit and the other a laborer. I turned on the recorder and peered through the viewfinder. It was working like a charm. Box after box of the illegal fish was hauled in the door and stacked along the wall. Tim, an Illinois investigator posing as a worker, was helping the pirates with the heavy boxes. When they were through, there was about 1500 pounds of black-market trout in the warehouse.

Tim began checking the shipment, and the boss outlaw stood at the desk waiting for his $2200 check from Tri State Foods. The suspects had their backs to Tim, who lifted the cover on the first box. He jumped back in mock surprise at what he saw in the carton. Tim is a real character and with that video equipment running he was going to have all of the fun he could. Overacting by about 300 percent, he started a routine that was about half Jackie Gleason and half W.C. Fields. He held up a giant lake trout in each hand and smiled at the camera like a proud fisherman. Then he pretended to take a big bite out of one of the wet slimy fish. I had to bite my tongue to stay quiet as I zoomed the lens in so that his smiling face filled the whole frame.

130

The crook was intently involved with a U.S. Fish and Wildlife agent who was pretending to be the warehouse foreman and was writing the check. The crook's laborer was lounging in a chair nearby and, for want of anything else to do, had begun picking his nose and wiping his fingers on his pants leg. This, of course, was too good to miss, so I zoomed the lens in on the action.

Remembering what I was supposed to be doing, I swung the viewfinder over and backed the lens off not a second too early to catch the outlaw taking the money for the evidence we had just purchased. There was more conversation and a promise to deliver more trout, and then they left.

Ten minutes later we were all doubled up with laughter, watching the rerun of Tim's performance and the nose-picking bandit. All of us, that is, except the U.S. Fish and Wildlife agent. He tried to deliver a lecture about the serious nature of our mission and how there was no room for foolishness. He got booed into silence halfway through his presentation. Eventually this guy wound up in the FBI, which is the perfect place for people who take themselves too seriously and have no sense of humor.

***

Bruce Gustafson was the chief of Michigan's undercover crew. He was a sharp officer and took his work very seriously, but he appreciated a good laugh, too. Gus had also acquired a videotape machine for his unit when they were involved in this investigation. He was working on some sport fishermen who were reported to be selling trout over on the east shore of Lake Michigan. It was legal to sell eggs from the female trout, but it was unlawful to sell the fish themselves. The eggs were bought by a company that bottled them and sold them for bait and, to a lesser degree, for caviar. In either case, a market was there and the fishermen were only too glad to get a few bucks for the eggs to defray the cost of their fishing trips.

When fishing was good, some of the anglers would catch a bag limit in the morning and then sell the fish to tourists and onlookers along the shore. Then they would go back out on the water and catch another limit to take home. This is called "double tripping" and is just as illegal as selling the fish. Several citizens had complained to the wardens about this activity. The Michigan wardens had tried to put a stop to the business. This, however, is one of those violations that is very difficult for uniformed officers to work, but is tailor-made for an undercover operation.

Bruce set up a pretty striped canopy tent near the pier and put a sign out front that said, "We buy eggs." His plan was simple. He would pay the going rate for eggs and then drop a subtle hint that he could also use the fish if the guy was inclined to sell them. He planned to run the deal for the remaining week of fishing season.

The plan was sound, but the major problem was going to be keeping track of the sellers for several months until it was time to take down Operation Gill Net. Here's where the video equipment would come in handy. If they could tape all of the transactions, they would have excellent evidence and could use the videotape to identify and help locate the suspects.

This was to be the first use of the new camcorder. Bruce located an old beat-up van that was still drivable. He painted the inside of the windows black except for the windshield. This way, nobody could see the cameraman working inside. The black paint also made the interior of the vehicle so dark that anyone looking in the front window would not notice the equipment. They could then set the camera up in the rear of the van and shoot the video through the windshield.

Bruce picked one of his newest agents to do the camera work. Although the guy was inexperienced, he was a bright kid who tried hard. Gus showed him how to operate the camera and had him park the van facing the tent so that the sales would be easily observed and recorded. The operation was ready for business.

Fishing was slow that morning, and Gus and his partner waited a long time for their first customer. Finally, a few fishermen began to straggle in. Bruce bought a few eggs. None of the fishermen picked up on his hint to buy fish, however. As the day wore on and the sun got higher, the temperature in the van began to climb. The black windows soaked up the sun's rays, and by early afternoon the rookie cameraman was sweltering in his cramped confinement. Although he was completely soaked in his own sweat and very uncomfortable, he wasn't going to give up his post and ruin the project — at least not as long as his new boss was buying the eggs, he wasn't.

Finally, things started to get more interesting. A tough-looking fisherman with three days' growth of beard showed up at the tent with four huge trout bulging with eggs. Bruce slit them open and extracted the eggs. Before he came to the part of his script where he would hint at a fish sale, the man was already offering to sell them to him.

In the van, the camera and the sweat were rolling. Being a little unfamiliar with the recorder, the kid rechecked the settings. He didn't want to miss this.

Bruce dickered price for a long time with the guy and finally a sale was agreed upon. The two men visited as Bruce put the fish in a large cooler on which he had been sitting and took out his wallet to pay for the fish. He appeared distracted by the conversation and returned his wallet to his pocket.

The warden in the van knew the transaction wasn't complete, so he kept the tape running. Bruce had the fish, but until the guy had the money they didn't have a case.

Once again Gus took his wallet out and started to thumb through it for the correct amount. Impatient for the deal to be made and anxious to get out of that oven, the rookie watched as Bruce again seemed to forget about paying the guy as their conversation continued.

After what seemed like an eternity, Bruce counted out the money into the culprit's hand. After the fisherman left, Bruce entered the van. "How did it go?" he asked. The rookie rewound the tape, switched on the monitor and the two men watched the replay of the illegal sale. Bruce noticed that the focus was nice and sharp and that the scene was always centered perfectly on the screen. The kid had done a good job.

As the action unfolded, the monitor emitted the sound of breathing. The sound function of the recorder had picked up the noises inside the van. Occasionally an unintelligible mumble could be heard from the monitor. The kid blushed. He didn't realize that the thing recorded sound, too. He was a little embarrassed at being caught talking to himself.

At last they came to the part where Bruce took out his wallet to pay the guy for the fish. When Bruce put his wallet away without completing the deal, a funny grunt came from the monitor. Later on, when Bruce aborted his second effort to pay the guy, a disgusted groan emitted from the speaker. By now the kid was in a full blush and unable to look at his boss.

Now, Bruce was pictured on the screen, standing with the bills in his hand and his hand down at his side. His new agent's voice boomed from the machine, "Give him the money, you stupid son of a bitch!"

Bruce Gustafson never would have made it with the FBI. He thought all of this was hilarious and enjoys telling the story. He says the new agent is a hell of a good man.

***

I got acquainted with a lot of different undercover people during Operation Gill Net. There were agents from five different jurisdictions involved in the project. With few exceptions, they were a hard-working, dedicated bunch. The hours and the working conditions got absolutely ridiculous from time to time.

When we had large shipments of legal fish to resell, they all had to be weighed, iced, repackaged and transported to market. We had no hired laborers, so it wasn't uncommon for investigators to work 18-hour shifts to get the perishable product properly handled so that we could recover our "buy money" and go out and do it all over again. There was little that was glamorous about nearly all of the work on the big fish case. It didn't take long to figure out what a man was made of under those conditions.

There was a pair of investigators on the project that really impressed me. They came to the warehouse in good humor every day. They always grabbed the dirty jobs and never complained about the work. That impressed me a little. What really impressed me a lot was their weird, flaky, dead-panned comedy routines.

Bill was slender and almost pale-looking. He had dark brown hair and very dark eyes. He grew his hair to shoulder length and cultivated a dark, drooping mustache. When he fixed a cold stare on you he bore a remarkable resemblance to Charles Manson. I think he realized it because he did it often.

Tim was a swinger. He seemed to have a lot more money than I did. For instance, he drove a fancy sports car or rode an expensive, fast motorcycle, depending on the weather. He also owned a Hobie Cat sailboat and a hot-air balloon. He was a cool, neat dresser and a good-looking guy. Colorful sayings and clever remarks flowed continually from his mind and mouth. He probably only bore a slight resemblance to Burt Reynolds before he started cultivating the coincidence. With a little effort, his mannerisms and cool attitude easily confused casual Reynolds fans.

Individually, Bill and Tim were talented, smart investigators.

When they were together, they were a comedy act that would have made them a lot of money in the right place. They seemed to know the words to every old '50s song and regularly harmonized for the warehouse crew, but I got the impression that they did it more for their own entertainment than ours.

Good, smart outlaws were always on the lookout for undercover people. This pair must have never been suspected. You might confuse them with many other types of people, but game warden was last on the list.

Lots of "U.C." people wanted to be like this pair, but I don't think anyone could learn to be like them. You had to be pretty flaky on a regular everyday basis to pull it off.

One day, they made a long trip in one of our trucks to pick up a load of illegal crappies from a Florida dealer. Once at their destination, they rented two rooms and then went out for a couple of beers. It got to be a little late before they went back to the motel.

Bill was concerned about their early meeting with the bandits the next morning. He was one of those sound sleepers. He told Tim that he would set his alarm, but that he often slept through it and wanted Tim to make sure that he didn't oversleep.

Sure enough, at seven in the morning Tim could hear Bill's alarm clock rattling away in the next room. It clattered for several minutes, so Tim called Bill's room on the telephone. The ringing phone joined the alarm clock in an awful din, but Bill slept on.

Tim, who slept in only his briefs, went out in the hall and over to his partner's door. Here he knelt down and began squeezing the entire contents of a can of lighter fluid through the crack under the door. It was about then that the door across the hall opened and a stylish, attractive lady stepped out of her room and into the hall. A gasp escaped her lips as she found Burt Reynolds kneeling in the hallway in his jockey shorts. Tim grinned and said, "Good morning, ma'am." Then he lit a match and shoved it under the door. There was a loud whoosh as a thin sheet of flame shot out into the hall and immediately vanished. The door flew open and there stood the nearly naked, wild-eyed image of Charles Manson. "I'M UP!" he shouted, and slammed the door in the faces of his partner and a lady who was getting her day off to a strange start.

Do you see what I mean? You can't practice stuff like that. You have to be natural at it. It is even harder to understand when you get to know them well and learn that these two are also very intelligent law enforcement officers. The flakiness is what made them good at "U.C." work.

***

Ken Decker was a federal agent. He was a skinny six-footer with a pronounced adam's apple and acute hyperactivity. He was constantly in motion. He could probably wear out a pair of jeans in a week, from the inside. He talked incessantly and invariably

136

about himself. He loved being a lawman and loved telling adventuresome, if imaginative, tales about his exploits. He also wrote his own press releases. When he busted a hunter for failure to sign his duck stamp, the news release sounded as if an ax murderer had been captured.

Ken was a U.S. Fish and Wildlife agent. They are sort of like game wardens, but not really. Most fish and game laws reside in state statutes and are enforced by state game wardens. The feds enforce only the migratory bird laws, the Lacey Act (which has to do with transporting critters across state lines), and some other miscellaneous acts.

Federal agent Decker was much more enthusiastic about himself than the confining limitations his enforcement position allowed. He rarely told his customers exactly whom he worked for. He usually just told them that he was a federal agent, and then let their imagination take it from there. When he wrote a ticket, the poor defendant often thought that he had been had by the CIA. I suppose this didn't really hurt anything. After all, the badges did look a little bit alike, and it sure made Ken feel a lot better.

About halfway through Operation Gill Net, Decker got wind of the investigation. He volunteered to help. He was told to show up at the Elgin office in grubby clothes at 10 o'clock one cold, snowy spring night. It was shortly before Lent and we were moving a lot of fish.

At 10:45 p.m., a van backed up to our loading dock and dropped off 40 boxes of perfectly legal whitefish. Each box contained about 65 pounds of fish, or roughly 20 of the slimy things. They weren't spoiled, but they were what the fishermen call "a little soft." We had a lot of money invested in this load and it was important that we turn them over to the market as quickly as possible. The problem was that the boxes all had the wrong company name on them and had been poorly packed. They were not properly iced and there was an inch of bloody slime in the bottom of every box.

The re-boxing and icing job was assigned to our new volunteer, federal agent Decker. I have to give him credit. He put on a rubber apron and tackled the task with enthusiasm. He dumped a box out on the floor and hosed down all of the fish with cold water. When they were rinsed clean, he shoveled a scoop of ice into one of our boxes and layered in the fish. When he had the box repacked he topped it off with another scoop of ice, put the cover on and moved the box into our cooler.

When he had three or four boxes done, one of the guys asked him, "You're packing them all with the right eye up, aren't you, Ken?" Decker looked puzzled and replied, "No, why?" Everyone else in the place had a puzzled look on their faces too, but Decker didn't notice.

"When we sell fish before a religious holiday they all have to be packed with the right eye up or else the rabbi won't accept them."

I don't think the practical joker thought it would go this far. He was probably as surprised as we were when Ken cussed a blue streak and brought his boxes out of the cooler, dumped them out on the floor and repacked the whole works with each fish on its left side, with the right eye up.

Federal agent Decker toiled on into the night beneath the veiled smirks of the investigators. He was a good worker. He handled the soft fish with tender care, and every single one had its right eye up. Eventually, my conscience started to bother me. When he was down to half a dozen boxes I stepped in and started to give him a hand. Once, I carelessly tossed one in the box wrong side up and he chewed on me like a first sergeant. To heck with him if he was going to act that way. I quit and let him finish by himself.

When the last box was in the cooler, everyone broke up with laughter as someone broke the news to Ken Decker. He was really steamed for a little while. He didn't like being made a fool, but it did make him feel like one of the boys. And, after all, he was the center of attention for a while.

We all scrubbed up, put on clean clothes and went out to a restaurant for breakfast. A pretty, smiling waitress came up and took our order. When she had it all written down, she looked at Ken, wrinkled up her nose and asked, "Have you been fishing already this morning?" We told him he had to sit at another table, but by then he wouldn't listen to anything we said.

***

I guess we ran out of storage space, money and ideas all at the same time. It was time to start contacting district attorneys in all of the counties where we had been working and start getting ready to serve warrants. Things went pretty well at first. Most of the prosecutors were surprised to hear what had been going on in their counties without their knowledge, but they were anxious to get going on the cases.

Nothing ever works perfectly, though. One prosecutor was really angry. She said that she took pride in being the chief enforcement officer in the county, and all of the other officers always let her in on undercover projects right from the start. Our apologies didn't seem to be smoothing her feathers at all and we were worried that she would throw out all of the deals we had made in her county, and there were a lot of good ones.

I don't know who's idea it was, but it was a stroke of genius. A new man was assigned to be our spokesman at the next meeting that was scheduled with her.

Terry Kelly worked undercover for one of the other states in this project. (Yes, I have changed the name to protect his identity.) He was too handsome for his own good. On top of his good looks, Kelly had a sweet smile, a soft voice and was very polite. Everywhere we went, the women dropped dead all around Terry. It was discouraging to eat with him in a restaurant. The waitresses fell all over him. I could hardly get their attention long enough to order. It was Terry Kelly who walked in the D.A.'s office at the next meeting.

Only two people know exactly what happened after that, and neither one of them is inclined to talk much about it. Anyway, in short order, Kelly and the D.A. were sharing sleeping accommodations, and she thought it was a wonderful idea to prosecute all of those nasty illegal fishermen. This arrangement lasted for several days, and we had warrants drawn up and made splendid plans for the great bust.

Terry started grumbling about how serious the woman was getting, and he was becoming nervous about his role in the case. After all, he was accustomed to only the finest, and while this woman wasn't ugly, she was no beauty queen. She was also making plans to make the arrangement permanent.

Eventually Terry decided it was getting too hot and he broke up with the lady. He hoped that the paperwork was far enough along that we wouldn't have any more problems with her. Apparently, his father failed to tell him "Hell hath no fury like a woman scorned."

She immediately iced the whole deal. She even came up with a pretty good reason. She had read in the newspaper about some toxic poisons which had been found in some fish taken from Lake Michigan. She said that when we were reselling fish for public consumption, we were effectively poisoning thousands of people, and she wasn't going to participate in the operation.

Terry Kelly was ordered by his supervisor to get back in bed with her and stay there until we had her cases on firm ground in the legal system. "Lord, that's a high price to pay," he replied .... but he did it.

***

When all of the smoke had cleared, we had bought just over 60,000 pounds of illegal fish. We collected about $175,000 in fines and several of the criminals went to jail. Many more commercial fishing licenses were revoked. We had broken the back of the blackmarket trout operations on the Great Lakes. As a result of the investigation, the statutes regulating commercial fishing were rewritten and the penalties were greatly increased. We were front page news in nearly every newspaper in 10 states.

Chapter 11

UNFINISHED BUSINESS

As a result of Operation Gill Net, Wisconsin's undercover squad enjoyed a good reputation among natural resource law enforcement agencies around the country. I regularly received calls from other states asking for information or recommendations about investigations they were conducting.

One day, the Department of Parks and Renewable Resources in Saskatchewan called. Their officers had been working on an outfitter who guided hunters in the southern part of the province. His name was Tony Murray. The Canadian officers said that he had no regard for closed seasons, bag limits or land owners' rights. He was a real thorn in the side of his neighbors as well as the provincial law officers.

At the time they called, Saskatchewan's department had no undercover enforcement program, yet they realized that the best way to shut down Murray was to have an agent hunt with him for a few days. After a lengthy phone conversation, I agreed to lend them two investigators for two weeks. Our agreement called for two Wisconsin agents with a vehicle and the necessary equipment. The Canadian agency provided background information on the suspect, enforcement authority for our officers and operating funds for the project.

Jack Beam and Tom Healin had both been with the "U.C." section for over a year. They had just completed a difficult investigation. The trip to Canada to pose as hunters sounded like a pleasant change of pace for them. I thought they would probably get some hunting in, and it should almost be like a paid vacation for them. Wrong again. They became involved in one of the most bizarre cases that any of us had ever worked.

Tom and Jack took a Dodge van and set out for Regina to meet the Canadian officers. The van had bogus Wisconsin license plates, which showed registration to the fictitious name maintained by Jack Beam. Both men used the false identification they had used on the previous case. They were well prepared and were working so far from home that it was a cinch that their true identities would not be discovered.

After a briefing with the provincial officers, the two wardens received non-resident hunting licenses and a wad of U.S. currency. They called Tony Murray on the phone and asked him if he could guide a couple greenhorns from the lower 48 for a week or so. They made arrangements to meet Tony at his home, several kilometers west of Regina.

In view of his nasty reputation, the investigators expected Murray to be an imposing figure. They were surprised to see that he was short and of slight build. He had long, reddish-brown hair and wore wire-rimmed glasses that sat crooked on his nose. He needed a bath. He was also half drunk. Murray offered them a drink of his homemade rhubarb wine. They had a glass with him and began talking details.

Tony wanted $150 a day and he guaranteed each of them a mule deer. They agreed on the price but told their guide that they wanted deer with big racks. They said they were trophy hunters. Tony said that big horns would be no problem. He took them into the living room and showed them two nice racks of horns that were mounted and hanging on the wall. He was very friendly towards the men and did not appear at all suspicious.

They met Murray's girlfriend. She was surly and unattractive. Obviously, her duties did not include housecleaning. The place was a pig pen. Half of the house was living room, which was a newer addition. The old part of the house contained a filthy kitchen and a bedroom. There were dirty clothes and dishes everywhere.

Over another round of wine, they planned the next day's hunt. The guide bragged about all of the deer he had killed and again assured them that they would get some real trophy deer. Tony's car was broken down, so they would use the van. There was no need for packed lunches, as they would return to town at noon. They would meet at the house early the next morning. Tom paid Murray the deposit he had requested, then the agents left. The wine bottle was empty and Murray was smashed.

Murray didn't look like a guide. He was wearing tattered blue-jeans and an old cotton shirt when they picked him up the next morning. His eyes were bloodshot behind his glasses. He had neither shaved nor bathed since they had left him the night before. He carried a rifle and another jar of rhubarb wine as he got in the van.

The first place the trio hunted was a series of little brush islands in a gigantic wheat field. Murray instructed Tom to drive through the crop of standing wheat towards the first patch of brush. They encountered a barbed wire fence. Tom stopped. Tony jumped out, took a pair of pliers from his hip pocket and cut the strands. He motioned Tom to drive through the gap. They continued on towards the brush, leveling a lot of good wheat as they went. When they were within a hundred yards of the first island of brush, a whitetail buck bolted from the thicket and started across the wheat field.

Murray shouted at Tom, "Hurry up. Step on it. Catch the son-of-a-bitch." Healin accelerated the van, but the field was so rough that they were tossed around in the cab. When it was obvious that they would not overtake the deer, Tony stuck the rifle barrel out the window and started shooting. The fourth shot dumped the buck in a heap.

The season for whitetails was closed. Our hunters had only mule deer tags. Murray hacked the head off of the carcass and said, "We'll get the trophies first and the meat later. Let's go." The carcass was left in the field to rot.

When they arrived back at the gap Murray had cut in the fence, there was an angry farmer waiting for them. He demanded to know who they were and why they had leveled hundreds of dollars' worth of his wheat. "I'll take care of him," Murray said, and he jumped out of the van with the rifle in his hand. He was like a crazy man. He raved that he would hunt anywhere he wanted to, and no farmer was going to stop him. He held the rifle in a ready position, gripping it so tight that his knuckles turned white. His language, which was normally profane, became absolutely vile. He looked perfectly capable of killing the farmer.

Soon the farmer backed down from the smaller man. Tony got back in the van and, as they drove away, he laughed long and hard at the farmer. These wardens were not new at this. They had worked on several difficult cases, but they agreed that Tony Murray was the most repulsive, obnoxious, anti-social individual either one of them had ever encountered.

The hunters had lunch in a small cafe in a nearby village. The place was busy, the food was good. The small dining room had several racks of deer horns hanging on the walls along with a pair of caribou horns. Murray bragged that he had killed the caribou during the closed season and had sold the horns to the owner of the cafe.

The guide told several stories during lunch and nearly always emphasized the unlawful aspects of his hunts. It was during one of these tales that he boasted that he was an expert with dynamite. He said that he used the explosive for blasting beaver dams and lodges. He claimed, too, to have worked as a professional blaster for years, blowing stumps and rocks out of the ground on land-clearing jobs.

Throughout the week that they hunted with Murray, the investigators carefully documented the locations, times and details of all of the violations committed by him. Whenever game was sighted, Murray became so excited that he quickly began shooting, rarely leaving any opportunity for his clients to shoot. Once while shooting at a running deer, he fired several shots that went directly into a small town a quarter of a mile away. Fortunately, no one was hit.

On another occasion he directed Jack to shoot at a deer standing in a grove of trees. Jack fired one shot that missed the deer. Murray fired instantly, dropping the deer in its tracks. This was the fifth deer he had killed that week. Murray did not have a hunting license.

While hunting geese later in the week, Murray again cut farm fences, saving a short walk to a pothole where geese had been feeding. Whenever they encountered landowners who questioned their presence or their activities, the wild-eyed little guide shouted them down. Murray always held his rifle in a threatening manner during these I "conversations," and everyone they met feared him.

Murray also killed pheasants during the closed season and shot ducks far in excess of the bag limit. He appeared to be unfamiliar with open seasons and limits on game. When the agents asked him about such matters, he laughed and said, "When you hunt with me you kill whatever you want to."

What I had hoped would be a pleasant break for Healin and Beam turned out to be a stressful and unpleasant assignment. They were spending 18 hours a day with the biggest slob they had ever seen. "U.C." wardens are used to associating with society's dregs, but Murray was the worst. They knew that the only way to really put him out of business was to gather as much evidence as possible against him, so the ugly slaughter continued. He was always drinking heavily and was invariably abusive to everyone they met.

When their work was completed, the investigators had documented over 60 separate serious violations against Tony Murray. They paid him, shook hands all around, and then reported to the Saskatchewan officials. After a lengthy debriefing, the provincial prosecutor was contacted and the necessary legal documents were completed.

Uniformed officers from the Department of Lands and Renewable Resources served papers on Murray and ordered him into court to be formally accused. At his initial appearance, Murray pleaded not guilty. He hired an attorney, probably with the guide fee he received from the officers, and a date was set for the trial.

Somehow, Murray, with the help of his girlfriend, raised bail money and Murray was released pending the trial. Jack and Tom returned home with the gracious thanks of the Province of Saskatchewan. They would have to return a month later for the trial.

About a week after Murray's initial court appearance, I received a phone call from the Royal Canadian Mounted Police. They had a warning for us. Murray's attorney had called the R.C.M.P. and told them that his client was making threats against the officials who were prosecuting him. Murray had repeated the threats often enough that his lawyer was convinced that he intended to attempt to carry them out. All efforts by the lawyer to dissuade Murray went unheeded. Specifically, the little guide intended to make two dynamite bombs. He said that with one he would blow up the Natural Resources office in Regina, and with the other he would "waste the two undercover agents that tricked me."

Tom and Jack had heard a lot of wild threats from defendants over the years. It is almost always a means for the crook to blow off steam and save face with his cohorts. They also knew Tony Murray pretty well by now and felt that this time it was different. This guy was completely capable of trying the stunt. Precautions would be taken when they returned to Regina for the trial.

About a week later, there was a loud explosion. Tony Murray's house was blown apart. The older portion of the house had a basement and that part of the building was scattered over a large area. The newer addition was standing, but damaged beyond repair. In that room the R.C.M.P. found two empty cartons marked "DuPont-Explosives." They were dynamite cases.

The mounties investigated for several days and called us regularly to keep us informed on their progress. Identifiable parts of Murray's body were found. His hands and feet, torn from his body by the blast, were found in separate locations in the basement. His head was in the back yard. Less than half of his body was recovered.

There was a car in the yard which Murray had recently rented. The odometer indicated that it had been driven only from the rental agency to Murray's yard. There was a bullet hole in a rear fender.

Murray's girlfriend was nowhere to be found. To this day her bank balance has never had another check drawn against it. None of her friends have ever seen her. She has simply disappeared.

Was it an accident or a suicide?

Was Murray making a bomb that went off accidentally?

Why the bullet hole in the rented car?

Is his girlfriend dead or alive?

Your guess is as good as any.

***

The bad guys were looking for us everywhere we went now. Although no names were ever mentioned, the press really made big news out of our recent successes. The commercial violators were well aware that we were active and were much more sophisticated than they had suspected. If one of the investigators pushed a little too hard, or asked one question too many, they were immediately accused of being who, in fact, they were. I suppose that many unsuspecting tourists were probably accused of the same thing just because they said the wrong thing in the right place.

To counter this problem, we hired two new investigators. One was a woman and the other a black. They were full-time officers with other police agencies but moonlighted with us on a part-time basis. They were effective from the start because they didn't look like any other wardens on the force.

The woman was pretty. Most outdoorsmen, and particularly the bad ones, have a lot of macho to maintain. An otherwise suspicious crook would readily deal with her, and she made several good cases. Men have been making fools of themselves over women for thousands of years. All we did was exploit the tendency.

Jerry Jackson was a nice guy. He was real popular with the other investigators and was a hard worker. He had a ready smile and used an open approach with his suspects. I sure did admire his nerve. It took lots of gumption for a black man to walk into those red-neck taverns up north and get accepted by the locals.

On the first case he was assigned, a bartender charged him 25 cents more for his tap beer than the other customers were paying. When he asked why, the barkeep said, "You're paying for the air conditioning, Smokey." He ordered a round of drinks for all of the patrons at the bar and said, "Drink up, boys, the beer may as well be on me, too." After that he paid the same price everyone else did.

Jerry was working on a guy named Gus Borowsky, who was selling deer in a small town in the western part of the state. Borowsky was a loner. He wasn't married and had few friends. He usually worked as a logger and often stayed in rooming houses or cabins near the job he was currently working on. Finding him wasn't going to be easy. Jerry (we called him J.J.) finally got word that Gus occasionally stopped in at Taylor's Bar and Grill and had offered to sell venison to other patrons in the bar.

J.J. spent most of the fall of 1986 in Taylor's Bar and Grill. It was a nice place as small town bars go, and he met a lot of people by hanging around in there. He played cards with one group and sometimes shot dice for drinks with two young guys who were regulars there. Jerry was the kind of guy who was fun to be around.

The proprietor of the place took a liking to J.J. They were both sports fans and used to make small, friendly wagers on a football game once in a while. It became an easy case to work, but he still hadn't met and made friends with Gus Borowsky.

One cold and stormy evening, Jerry walked in and found the place empty except for the owner. He pulled up his favorite stool and ordered a beer. The two men swapped jokes for nearly an hour. J.J. was still the only customer and he decided that, as bad as the weather was, he was probably wasting his time.

About the time he was going to leave, the door opened and a blast of cold wind and a tall grumpy-looking man entered. He saw J.J. and said, "Are you serving niggers in here now?" Mr. Taylor said, "I'm sure serving this one. He's a friend of mine." The big, dirty newcomer took a seat three stools from Jerry and ordered a shot of brandy and a glass of beer. He sat glaring at J.J. as he sipped his drink. Pretty soon, he started harassing Jerry. At first, it was just wise remarks, but soon it got racial and nasty. Jackson ignored him for a while. Eventually it became apparent that this would continue to escalate until something physical took place.

When the bigot poked J.J. with his index finger, he suddenly found himself with his arm twisted up behind his back and his face in a puddle of beer on the bar. He groaned a curse and tried to pull free. When the guy tried to move, Jackson twisted the arm a little higher and watched the big man stand up on his toes, trying to relieve the pressure on his wrist and shoulder.

Taylor said, "That's pretty neat. Can you hold him like that while I get the door open?" The bartender pushed the door against the icy blast and stood out of the way as J.J. took the guy by the collar with his free hand, shoved the obnoxious jerk across the room and dumped him out into the street. Taylor and Jackson sat quietly at the bar finishing the last of their drinks. Jerry asked the proprietor, "Who in hell was that creep?" The owner said that he was just a bum who stops in once in a while. "His name is Gus Borowsky."

J.J. stopped in my office the next morning and told me that he had finally met the suspect, but hadn't exactly befriended him. He guessed that I would have to give the case to a different investigator.

***

Federal agent Decker tried a little undercover work on a ginseng case he was assigned. Ginseng is a little plant that grows wild in shaded woods. It has a small berry on top and roots like a pale,

150

miniature carrot on the bottom. Those who can recognize it dig it up, dry it and sell it to dealers. It takes a lot of it to make a pound, but if you find that much, it will bring nearly $200.

The stuff is also cultivated domestically, but the domestic variety has a slightly different appearance and is not as effective. It's only worth about half as much as the wild stuff. Most folks will tell you that, in reality, none of it is worth a plug nickel. You see, it's supposed to be an aphrodisiac. There are very few people in this country who believe in the plant, especially at $200 a pound. The Orientals think it's marvelous, however. I guess it's the Chinese answer to our old snake oil remedies. They swear that it cures everything from fits and farts to freckles. Nearly all ginseng harvested in this country is exported to the Orient.

Here is where federal agent Decker entered the scene. Anything which is both wild and gets exported is regulated by the feds. There is a permit required and reports that must be made out and submitted with each shipment.

As best I can recall, there was a guy that was shipping "sang," as the diggers call it, without a permit. He was dealing in both the wild and the domestic plant and was a pretty good businessman. He was a Japanese citizen living in this country. He had very good contacts back in Japan and was easily selling all of the root that he could buy. He'd made enough money in a very short period of time to buy a beautiful new home in a better part of town. He did most of his buying out of his home or out of the back of a small pickup truck, and he wasn't bothering with any silly federal permits or reports. Federal agent Decker got wind of the operation.

Decker planned to pose as a digger and take some root to the guy's house. He figured that he could engage the guy in a long conversation, get a look at all of the roots in his house and truck and return later with a search warrant. He hoped to seize thousands of dollars worth of ginseng and clamp the dude in irons. He hid a small tape recorder in his left cowboy boot and his snubnosed .38 in the right one. He was ready to become a covert operator.

If I know him, he had the press release in rough draft form before he walked up the sidewalk and rang the doorbell. A small, smiling oriental man opened the door and politely greeted him. They stood on the steps and talked briefly about the selling price of ginseng. There was no invitation to enter the house. Instead, the little man directed Decker out to the rear of the pickup truck parked in front of the garage door.

Although he was friendly, he was all business, and Ken had little luck trying to extend the conversation along more informal lines. In just a minute or two, the guy had weighed the ginseng on a small scale that was in the back of the truck and had written a check for the agent.

This wasn't going very well. The transaction was done and Decker hadn't even been close to getting in the house to look for the contraband root. The federal agent had an inspiration.

As the two men stood talking, Decker began squirming and shifting his weight from one foot to the other. He pinched his knees together and bent forward slightly at the waist. With a pained look on his face he feigned a full bladder and asked the suspect about the possibility of using the bathroom. The gracious man quickly consented and Decker hurried towards the front door in his wonderful imitation of a man about to wet his knickers.

Just as he reached for the knob, the little oriental called out to him. "I'm sorry sir, but it is a custom with my people and you must leave your shoes outside on the step." Ken contemplated the hardware in his boots for a second and gave up. "I guess I don't have to go so bad that it won't wait until I get home," he said, and strode to his car, got in and drove off.

Chapter 12

THE FAT LADY SINGS

A few weeks ago, I rummaged around in the closet and found my dress uniform. I brushed the dust from the shoulders of the coat and ironed the hanger crease out of the pants. I was pleased to find out that it still fit pretty well. Because of my undercover assignment, I hadn't had it on in 10 years. In a few days I would retire and I wanted to have a picture taken.

It had a really familiar feel to it. I straightened my tie in front of the mirror and the old memories began to return. I recalled how proud I was the first day I wore it. I wrote a guy a ticket for motor-trolling that day. He was from Minnesota and did his best to convince me that he was really too important to be getting a ticket. He said he was a retired police chief and was acquainted with several legislators in that state.

He wrote a letter to Wisconsin's governor and complained that the new game warden up north was chasing all of the tourists out of the state. Governor Reynolds responded and I received a copy of the memo. I still have it. The copy machines of those days were pretty poor. The paper is brown now and the printing is just a little darker brown. It's hard to read. He told the complainer that he was welcome to come back and fish here again if he thought he could follow our rules. If not, maybe he'd better fish somewhere else. I was proud as hell.

I remembered standing up in Judge Cooper's court wearing that gray suit and swearing to tell the truth, the whole truth and nothing but the truth. Then I did, and the judge believed me. This time he put the Sanderson brothers in jail for 30 days. I'd had them in his court so many times he was sick and tired of only fining them. I was proud as hell.

Louie Simmons was a popular old-time game warden who retired before I went to work. I'd never met him but I'd heard lots of stories about him. When he died, my boss told me to put on a clean uniform and some white gloves. There were going to be six game wardens carrying Louie's remains to the grave, and I would be one of them. We stood at attention while a kid from the high school band played "Taps" on his coronet. He wasn't good, but it still sent a shiver up my back.

Some gray-headed old guys from the VFW fired their rifles on command. I guess they were supposed to shoot in unison but they were pretty ragged. It sounded more like the first few seconds of the opening of duck season on Clam Lake. It's the thought that counts, though. The whole affair gave me a big lump in my throat. I looked at those other five guys in gray and thought, I'll bet Louie would have been proud as hell. I know I was.

It's funny how our merciful memories dredge up only the winners. By the time I quit daydreaming, I was nearly blubbering. I got in the car and drove to town for the photo session.

When it was over, I stopped in the grocery store to pick up a few things. I probably wouldn't even have been there except that it felt good to be walking around in the uniform that I was so proud of. I went down an aisle looking for the oatmeal and met a pretty lady pushing a shopping cart with one hand. There was a cute little girl about four years old holding on to the other hand and toddling alongside of her. I heard the kid ask, "Is he a policeman, Mommy?" The lady said, "No, he's worse than a policeman. He's a game warden." You can bet the farm that someone she knows well has paid one of our tickets.

Yeah, I was somewhat deflated. I remembered then that it was often like that. That stuff comes on the same day and in the same box that the uniform does. If you work hard and do a good job, you can be certain that somebody is going to be mad as hell about it.

Harold Hettrick was the assistant chief warden. He'd been a good warden with a full career in the field before his promotion. Now, he was doing a lot of good things in the headquarters office.

There are several wildlife exhibits in the state. The department licenses these fenced areas where wild animals are kept in captivity, usually as tourist attractions. We require that the conditions at the exhibits are sanitary and humane. Otherwise, we don't have much regulatory effect on them.

The brass in the headquarters office started getting phone calls and letters about critters being neglected and poorly cared for at some of these places. Harold Hettrick decided to do something about it. He sent a letter to every warden who had an exhibit in his area and instructed him to go and inspect the facility, their records and the condition of the animals. He said to bust anyone who was not complying with the license law or was mistreating his stock.

The response to the letters was excellent. The wardens found several places where there were real problems. In some cases, the dependent wildlife was being left for days without water. Several starving animals were found and some really filthy pens and enclosures located during the inspections. In the court cases that followed, many of the licenses were revoked and the animals were sold or released. Other exhibits were cleaned up and regularly monitored following the crack-down. It was a good stroke of business.

Just outside Hayward, there was a busy little tavern called The Ranch. It was owned and operated by a woman with a heart of gold. Her personality was what made the place hum. She had a quick wit and a spicy vocabulary. Her name was Vivian and she had an opinion on everything, which she usually expressed with sarcastic vulgarity.

Vivian liked game wardens. Her place became sort of a watering hole for wardens passing through that corner of the country. We'd had several parties there and she would lock up the joint and give it to us for these occasions. It's safe to say that the wardens in the northwest area of Wisconsin liked Vivian, too.

She had a wildlife exhibit license and had two or three deer in a fence behind her tavern. She enjoyed feeding and watching them, and I suppose they did attract a little additional business to the place.

Wildlife exhibit licenses expire on the last day of the calendar year. Viv picked a bad time to forget to send in her renewal fee. Harold's cleanup of the wildlife exhibits was in full swing. Hettrick was checking the license records and discovered that hers was delinquent. He sent a letter to the young warden in Hayward and told him to go write Vivian a ticket for the infraction.

This was going to be the toughest ticket this kid had written. He talked it over with the other guys and they decided that they would all chip in and pay the fine themselves.

When the warden explained to Vivian that he just hated to write the ticket, that it really wasn't his idea and that the guys were going to pay the fine for her, she hit the ceiling. How in the devil could some "desk-bound bureaucrat" from an office 250 miles away tell one of her game wardens to pinch her? She raved on about how well her deer were cared for and insisted that this license deal was just something that she had forgotten to do.

She felt just terrible, but not as terrible as her local game warden did. It felt to him as if he was arresting his mom. Viv told him not to feel bad, she understood whose fault it was. She locked the door and opened two beers. They sat on opposite sides of the bar and drank to their misery. The more they talked and drank, the worse they felt. The worse she felt, the madder Viv got. She asked the warden who this guy was who had ordered the bust, but he knew better than to give her the name. At least he knew better until about the fifth beer. She promised him she would never tell where she found out, and he gave in.

He was surprised when she immediately picked up the phone and had the operator connect her with the department's state head-quarters down in Madison. In just a moment she was giving Hettrick a piece of her mind. It went on for the longest time. She hardly stopped for breath. Harold tried at first to calm her down but he couldn't get a word in edgewise. Finally, after he thought he had been called every derisive name he'd ever heard, she gave Harold the floor.

The first thing he asked was, "Where did you get my name?" She said, "I just called that fancy office and told the receptionist that I wanted to talk to the stupidest bastard in the place, and she put you on the line." Then she hung up. You did a good job, Harold, but somebody got mad about it.

Well, anyway, I started to tell you about my retirement. They had a heck of a nice party for me, complete with handshakes from the guys and hugs from the gals, and they really overdid it on the gifts.

It wasn't just a job, it was a way to live. It was something that you were, more than something that you did. After nearly 28 years of it, it feels strange now to be . . . just me. It was a good way to live and, often, it was a lot of fun. Busting folks isn't fun but "getting there" often is. I hope I did some good along the way. In spite of the shortcuts and liberties that we sometimes took, it's good, honest work that needs to be done. It feels good to be one of those who did it. It's too bad about all the folks we had to offend, but that's the nature of the job. I'm not going to apologize for that.

Well, maybe I'll go look up that lady and her daughter I met in the grocery store. I'll tell them that I used to be a game warden, but I'm OK now.

ABOUT THE AUTHOR

Jim Palmer was born in Spooner, Wisconsin and graduated from Wisconsin State University-Superior in 1963. He served with the Wisconsin Conservation Department, later renamed the Wisconsin Department of Natural Resources, from 1961 until his retirement in 1989.

He was a game warden, pilot, covert investigator and chief of the Special Investigations Section. In 1988 he was recognized as the Wisconsin Wildlife Officer of the Year.

He lives and writes at his home in the mountains above Silver City, New Mexico.

160